I0490989

ONE

GIANT

ONE

STONE

MICHAEL A. WOODS

WESTBOW
PRESS®
A DIVISION OF THOMAS NELSON
& ZONDERVAN

Copyright © 2022 Michael A. Woods.

All rights reserved. No part of this book may be used or reproduced by any means, graphic, electronic, or mechanical, including photocopying, recording, taping or by any information storage retrieval system without the written permission of the author except in the case of brief quotations embodied in critical articles and reviews.

WestBow Press books may be ordered through booksellers or by contacting:

WestBow Press
A Division of Thomas Nelson & Zondervan
1663 Liberty Drive
Bloomington, IN 47403
www.westbowpress.com
844-714-3454

Because of the dynamic nature of the Internet, any web addresses or links contained in this book may have changed since publication and may no longer be valid. The views expressed in this work are solely those of the author and do not necessarily reflect the views of the publisher, and the publisher hereby disclaims any responsibility for them.

Any people depicted in stock imagery provided by Getty Images are models, and such images are being used for illustrative purposes only. Certain stock imagery © Getty Images.

Scripture taken from the King James Version of the Bible.

ISBN: 978-1-6642-6471-7 (sc)
ISBN: 978-1-6642-6472-4 (hc)
ISBN: 978-1-6642-6470-0 (e)

Library of Congress Control Number: 2022907700

Print information available on the last page.

WestBow Press rev. date: 10/14/2022

CONTENTS

1

———◦———

DEFINE

For the last thirty years, I have been searching to discover the core precepts that guide good leadership. As a young man in the navy, I was perplexed by the random distribution of leadership talent. Sailors lined up to follow some leaders, while other leaders of the same rank could not keep a crew of subordinates involved long enough to sweep a deck. I wanted to know where leadership comes from and how it manifests in the world around us.

I have met some people who are natural-born leaders. From birth, they possess the personality, charisma, and drive to motivate a team. People seem helpless in their presence to do anything other than grab a piece of rope and start pulling. Team members are so glad to be included that they never feel coerced or manipulated. And the rewards of being on these teams as they drive toward the leader's defined conclusion are more internally satisfying than any six-figure paycheck. Of these leaders, I have seen only a handful.

Unlike these natural leaders, I had to study and practice to figure out how to lead. Over the last thirty years, I have searched out leadership's foundational precepts and their applications. Like anything worth pursuing, it has taken me a long time to get to the point of authoring this book, and the discoveries along the way ranged from uncomfortable to quite painful. Yes, I made a lot of mistakes in thirty years of searching, and I will share some with you. Fortunately for you, though, this book is not about me. It is about the precepts that determine your success as a leader. Applying these precepts will not prevent mistakes, but it will give you the tools to get your team back on track after one.

Let us start simply and at the beginning. Leadership begins when you choose to lead.

DAVID AND GOLIATH

While the story of my life may not be a good analogue, often these precepts need to be demonstrated to allow us to see their proper application. To that end, I have chosen another leader, whose accomplishments are well documented in the Bible, to act as our example. King David has always been a favorite historical figure of mine. Though David himself is the example leader, I found one event in his life most instructive—the day he faced Goliath. The basic precepts I want to share with you are amply demonstrated in this short account in 1 Samuel 17. About ten years ago, I began studying this story of a day in the life of David, and this book is a collection of leadership precepts and their applications that I have found demonstrated in this account.

Before getting to the battle in the valley of Elah, let us set some guidelines for our analogy. Words are the guides we need, defined for this context so that there is no misunderstanding. For instance, the words *precept* and *application* have specific meanings given to them by experts who compile dictionaries. But there may be nuances and subtle backstories that give color to their meaning in this context. Clear definitions ensure our success in communication.

Precepts are general rules intended to direct thoughts and actions. Most dictionaries I have consulted put the order as actions and thoughts, but that reverses cause and effect. Leadership precepts are those rules that determine how one person can get another person or group to do work in unison for a common goal. The precept guides and directs the thoughts and defines the proper realm for the actions, but thought should always precede action.

Precepts guide your thoughts and actions but knowing them is not a guarantee of success. They must be applied. *Application* is defined as making decisions based on precepts that guide the team in accomplishing the leader's vision. Not all leadership is effective. I can attest to the results that come from ignoring precepts or, worse, from deliberately misapplying them. The precepts always work when applied, but the motivations and vision of the leader are not always in the best interests of the follower. In these cases, great harm can be done, and in the end, the leader is destroyed, so I would counsel against misusing these precepts. If you need examples of how devastating the leader's destruction can be, think of Hitler, Saddam Hussein, or Jezebel (if you are not familiar with her death, check it out in the Bible in 2 Kings 9:30–37). The precepts work for bad leaders, but the results of misapplied leadership are not desirable. Effective leadership that brings success, prosperity, and long life to everyone on the team requires a leader's proper attention to applying them.

The word *vision* is not referring to some spiritual or psychedelic manifestation of the future. Vision is a clearly defined change in the world that the leader is attempting to create. Do not think that because the leader is the originator and keeper of the vision that they should get all the credit for the accomplishment. While the leader's determination implants and keeps the vision continually in the team's collective thinking, this action by the leader only creates buy-in from the team. They must accept the vision as their goal. Only when the entire team sees and seeks to accomplish this vision can it be manufactured. The team makes it happen, not the leader. The vision is only the starting point.

CHOOSE

What is the first precept? A leader must first choose to lead. Good or bad leadership is all you will find; there is no indifferent leadership. The common expression "whatever" is never uttered by a leader. An indifferent leader would lead his or her followers directly to the unchosen destination of nowhere. An effective leader has made a choice to deliberately guide a team to change the world. A leader wants to succeed in creating a vision, needs a team to do so, and decides to lead.

A leader must first choose to lead. The statement is simple, but before you start defining your vision, consider the consequences. Not all the precepts I will show you result in pleasant outcomes for the leader. Some of them will break the leader's heart, leave the leader isolated even from the team, and, in cases of great opposition, lead to failure for the team. These burdens are often taken too lightly when making the decision to lead. If you are not prepared to deal with the unpleasantness that comes from leadership, your vision will blur under the strain and your team will stumble and fall. Failure is always a possibility, but only when it is not an option will a leader have any hope of surviving a vision's creation. There are some unpleasant times ahead. Be prepared before you choose to lead.

Application of this precept is not hard. Choose. If you are reading this book, then you have already begun thinking about a situation in your life/world where you would like to create a change. In the end, that is what leaders do; they create change in the world around them. If the leader is deliberate, expresses a clear vision, and properly applies the precepts, then the change is likely to be an improvement. But the first step is always the choice.

Consider another precept. Every decision supports someone's vision. This may seem like an overly broad statement that can be easily disproved. But take a few hours or days to think it through. When you purchase a pack of gum at the gas station, how does that decision support someone's vision? If your motivation was to make sure the onions you had at lunch did not impact the conversation you would need to have with a team member that afternoon, then you were leading. You might like the flavor of this gum, but then you are responding to the leadership of the marketing team that designed the flavor, packaging, shelf position, and price that put the gum where you needed it. Take some time to consider and see if you can make one decision that is not governed by this precept of leadership. If the choice is not furthering the vision your team is working on, then who are you following and toward what vision?

Every decision supports someone's vision. Applying this precept means that, as the leader, you need to know how each decision supports another leader's vision or creates movement in your team to accomplish your chosen vision. Do not assume that your vision needs to be different from your leader's vision. You do not need to be the origin of the vision to lead people to accomplish it. All that is required is the choice to lead a team to accomplish the vision but be aware that every choice you make in life is in support of a leader's vision. With careful deliberation, that vision will be yours.

This precept is not the only one concerning decisions. Consider also that decisions have consequences for the leader, the team, and the people they encounter. Think of it like driving a car. Every twitch of the wheel or change in pressure on the gas pedal has potential life-or-death consequences for the driver, the passengers, and the other drivers on the road. Combine this precept that decisions have consequences with some of the other precepts that we will cover, and, choosing to lead might seem like driving your new car through the middle of a demolition derby in reverse while blindfolded. Make sure the vision is worth risking the potential consequences.

These precepts operate as a collective of perspectives. The application of only one precept is not likely sufficient to inform your decisions. Knowing and applying all the precepts to every decision is what successful leadership looks like. If this seems like an impossible task, then take care when choosing to lead. You may still be forced to choose the leadership role but be aware of the burdens it will create for you. My favorite verse in the Bible says, "See then that ye walk circumspectly, not as fools, but as wise" (Ephesians 5:15). The word *circumspectly* means seeing a situation from every possible angle and considering every possible consequence of a decision. This is what a leader must do. The precepts only provide a framework that allows a leader to make effective decisions quickly.

Making effective decisions becomes imperative when you circumspectly consider the possible consequences those decisions create for the team you are leading. Those are real people who are following your leadership, and your choices will impact their lives. Make the wrong decision, and they could end up dealing with adverse consequences. If you are not serving your team by making good decisions, they will not support your vision for long. Since your vision cannot be accomplished without them, take great care with each decision. Be circumspect. Especially when choosing to lead.

DEFINITIONS

Your decisions will have many precepts that guide the outcomes, but I will be using five other words that should be defined before we get to the other precepts: authority, responsibility, accountability, delegation, and permission. These are the backbone concepts that underlie the mechanics of how effective leadership works. These are often poorly defined and more regularly misapplied in our world today, so I need to give some clarity before we go any further.

Authority

Authority is the power to make a decision and see to it that the decision is carried out. This power over other people can have many focuses: money, physical strength, intelligence, charisma, social/political position, a delegation from a higher authority, and even willingness to do violence. The important perspective here is that all decisions are governed by authority, and as a leader, if you do not have the authority, you will need to get it before you can act.

The most often missed aspect of authority is its true origin. Within most of the world's systems, money and/or position might be identified as the source of authority. But everyone answers to someone for their actions and has had authority delegated to them by others. Authority is hierarchical by nature but is not spontaneously generated. There is a source, the Creator. God decides who shall have what authority, and for His reasons.

We will talk more about obtaining authority in chapter 4. For now, simply consider that even misused authority has been delegated down the chain of command, and this delegated authority, the power to make and uphold decisions, originates at the top of the hierarchy with God. "Let every soul be subject unto the higher powers. For there is no power but of God: the powers that be are ordained of God" (Romans 13:1). There are some deep theological concepts in this verse that I will not cover in this book; however, before you choose to lead and exercise authority, you should know where it comes from.

A word of warning: gaining authority through the willingness to do violence is an often-used method of gaining authority without a delegation. Violence need not be physical or life-threatening. The violence could be psychological, financial, or social in nature. Threatening a team member with expulsion if they do not do as you command is one example. The opposite of that would be team members threatening to quit if the leader does not change some aspect of the vision. (For this, the leader must refuse to accept fear and push ahead to the goal even if the threatened action becomes real.) The threat of violence generates fear in the followers and forces them to take actions as directed, but they will never contribute beyond following orders. Fear of violence always has an object of the person willing to commit it, which breeds resentment instead of buy-in. Teams that are led by fear are always one step away from rebellion and insurrection. The spark in the tinder is one person who refuses to be afraid.

Responsibility

Responsibility is the opportunity to make independent decisions. Typically, within a team, each member will have an arena of decisions that they are given the opportunity to make. While they are allowed to operate independently within their arena, council from other decision-makers is often critical to overall team success. Most often, responsibility is an extension of authority, at least when these concepts are properly applied. As the leader, you often assume responsibility rather than wait for it to be assigned to you. You are choosing to lead or choosing to make yourself responsible for seeing a change take place.

Accountability

Accountability is the state of accepting credit for the consequences of a decision. Every decision has consequences for the leader, the team, and the people they encounter. Those consequences may be good or bad, and occasionally both, depending on your part in the change that was created. This concept also has two perspectives since the accountable party may accept credit in their own thoughts or may accept credit attributed by others. Either way, the accountable party has some consequences, internal or external, to deal with resulting from the decision that was made.

Accepting the consequences of decisions is different from dealing with the consequences of actions. While leaders should hold themselves accountable for decisions made by their followers, those followers remain accountable for their actions. Effective leaders must learn to separate the results of decisions made from the way they were implemented.

Misapplied Concepts

These concepts that underpin leadership precepts are commonly misplaced in our world. Though I see it most often in business, these sour consequences can be seen in every team environment. Before I share with you the proper alignment of these concepts by defining *delegation*, you may find it instructive to consider the consequences of the possible misplacements.

Authority is most often misplaced when it is held by the leader and not shared with team members. This situation is quite common in businesses where the boss makes all the decisions, and the workers do what they are told. While this may be effective in the short-term accomplishment of a few daily objectives, the team's success is limited by the number of decisions that the leader can make. The leader only has so many hours in a day that can be given to making decisions. When that maximum is reached, team members queue up and wait their turn to be heard and have a decision made. The leader falls further and further behind on the decisions, opportunities pass, situations change without a decision being made, and the vision falls apart.

Teams where the leader retains all authority stand out. The team members are always apathetic since they cannot change the situation without the authority to do so. If asked what they are working on, each will tell you they are waiting for a decision to be made, and until then, there is not much they can do except keep up with the day-to-day. The team is angry with the leader because team members know what to do to move forward but are not allowed to do anything but wait. The leader will spend most of the day at their desk reading emails. In fact, the leader will get so many emails in a day that they cannot read them all (I have some email advice at the end of this chapter). Tracking the number of emails you regularly receive, is a good measure for making sure you are not holding too much authority.

In the end, the leader becomes a tyrant, lashing out at the apathetic team attempting to make them do their jobs. The team's vision is lost in the constant reassessment of procedures. These reassessments never result in any real changes because change requires a decision, and the leader is too busy blaming the team for failure to make any more decisions. A new leader is the only way to break the stalemate.

The companion mistake to misapplied authority is making people responsible without giving them the authority to make the decisions. Apathy will be replaced with downright hostility in these teams. People will attempt to get decisions made by trying to handoff responsibility to other team members. These handoff attempts create territory battles that often lead to intense arguments over what to do. Without any authority to decide, team members walk away from arguments only to return to the same argument several days later.

These organizations, when viewed from the outside, are quite hostile. The hostility usually spills out into the world outside the team as members seek a solution. While passionate debate is always a part of good team decision-making, the arguments should always end with a team consensus and a decision based on authority. If an action item from one meeting is the same as an action item from the previous meeting, and that action item is to revisit the question in the next meeting, then responsibility without authority is at play.

This leads to the most misapplied of the concepts, accountability. Who gets credit for the situation? Or more specifically, who is to blame? An ineffective leader who is holding the team accountable will always blame the team members when the vision wavers. If the leader accepts no accountability but is still holding all the authority, they will blame their leaders for not providing enough resources to fulfill the vision.

The team members who have no authority know the leader is to blame. Those team members who at least have responsibility blame other team members to avoid having anyone hold them accountable. These organizations are crippled, and the most common response to any question is, "That's not my fault!" Pass the buck, blame corporate, accuse the weather, lambast your customer, but make sure you hand off the accountability, or you become the next scapegoat. These organizations are full of secretive, hostile people trying to protect themselves from the consequences of being blamed while also making sure that someone else becomes the next sacrifice.

Organizations that spend their time holding team members accountable develop rigid policies that dictate behavior but never focus on the vision. Team members spend their entire day discussing the irrational policies with other team members and discovering ways to make sure they are not blamed when things go wrong. If something does go right, the leader will take all the credit, but usually, things go wrong, and heads roll. When team members are dismissed because they did not follow the rules, every other team member will clam up, toe the line, and never make another decision for fear of violating a policy.

During the early months of COVID-19, I noticed an explosion of evidence indicating that most businesses suffer from this instance of holding team members accountable. As the stay-at-home orders were issued, companies scrambled to establish work-at-home scenarios that would keep their people working. Suddenly, every company became interested in technologies that would facilitate these at-home workers. Application of technology for this purpose centered on how remote workers could be held accountable for how they spent their time. Businesses deployed cameras, pressure-sensitive chairs, keystroke analyzers, and AI that could determine if someone worked or played while in their home office. Managers suddenly had a new problem of how to hold team members accountable for doing enough work rather than empowering them to make decisions.

These organizations are being led by individuals who are still playing school. Do you remember that game we played as kids? "OK, class, I am the teacher. You have to do what I say. Face forward, both feet on the floor, keep your eyes on your own paper, and no laughing or having fun." These teams have forms for every situation that fully document what is being done so that when a mistake is discovered, we will know who is at fault. Every vertical surface in the breakroom has a rule posted to it, as do the hallways and bathrooms. The most important piece of equipment in the office is the time clock, and it is checked several times a day. Members are held accountable for the hours they work and not for the work they get done. The leader spends all their time enforcing the rules by scolding and disciplining the offenders. If your boss has a star chart on the wall where they give gold and silver stars for not breaking the rules … run.

If you are on that team, you are living in a constant state of fear, a fear founded on the sure knowledge that the blame will come to you someday. You have two options to correct this situation: choose to lead or run. If you choose to lead, you will find it easy to gain responsibility from your teammates if you step up and accept accountability. The downside is that you will now get the blame for everything that is going wrong, so be ready to ask for the authority, or you have made yourself the next scapegoat. If you are not ready to lead, get out now. Do not spend another day working on a team that has no vision other than self-implosion. Leave quickly and quietly.

Delegation

One solution to all these poor-functioning teams is proper delegation. Leaders must first acquire the authority needed to make decisions. Then the leader must assign portions of that authority in even measure with responsibility. This cannot be ambiguous. The delegation of authority and responsibility must be well defined and transparent so that the entire team understands who has the authority and responsibility to decide. Then accountability stays with the leader. Please do not miss this point. As the leader, you must remain accountable for how your authority is used. When you delegate that authority effectively to the correct team member, you will be accountable for the good decisions they make. If you delegate too much authority without responsibility, you are accountable for creating a tyrant. Give responsibility without authority, and you are accountable for the hostile team member. Try to hold your team accountable, and you will waste your time trying to enforce rules that are designed to govern behavior, not accomplish a vision. The leader is always accountable.

Consider the decision math. Your team can grow and move forward only to the limit of the number of decisions that can be made in a day. There will always be more decisions to make than you can get to in one day. When you hold team members accountable, they stop making decisions. If the decisions are not made, you will be held accountable. Therefore, you must allow your team members to make decisions, and you must remain accountable for those decisions. As the leader, you will spend most of your time making decisions about this delegation, and only occasionally will you make strategic decisions about how to accomplish the vision. Your team will be the ones who make day-to-day tactical decisions and build the vision.

If this level of accountability is not for you, then back away from the leadership decision. If you do not have it in you to trust team members with that much of the decision-making, get ready to work a lot of long hours making decisions that will eventually overwhelm you and lead to failure. The precepts I want to share will help you make more effective decisions faster, but you will not be able to make them all. You will be teaching these precepts to your team and relying on them to make decisions you are pleased to be accountable for.

Permission

Another seemingly effective alignment of the concepts of authority, responsibility, and accountability leads to the concept of permission. Permission is the temporary assignment of authority, responsibility, and accountability to act on a single decision. Permission replaces delegation for leaders who are building a power hierarchy instead of an authority hierarchy. Increasing the leader's power is the only vision that matters, though team members are often recruited by presenting them with a smoke screen vision that inspires them to join the team. Joining the team requires team members to submit their authority, responsibility, and accountability to the leader, who then hoards them for the purpose of growing their power base. The power side of authority becomes the focus of the few decisions that are made, and though the number of decisions is limited, they are tightly focused.

If the leader's power base is large enough and they are highly placed enough in an authority hierarchy, then the team may from time to time take swift and decisive action in a campaign to accomplish a vision. Accomplishment will increase the leader's power, which appears to everyone to be a side effect of the successful campaign. Successive successful campaigns reveal a pattern that establishes the increase in power as the only motivation for the campaigns. While increasing power is seldom expressed as the reason for the campaigns, they do still accomplish that objective, so this can be considered an effective leadership method pragmatically. It can produce the desired result.

I will wait until chapter 10 to present details of the power-driven leadership approach because it has a devastating downside. Failure in a campaign destroys the delicate balance of power that keeps the hierarchy together. Each time the leader commits to a campaign, they risk everything, and failure will mean starting over again. Imagine spending fifty years building a power base that allows you to take a substantial risk on a worthwhile campaign and the effort fails. Though you are now more experienced, it will still take as much time to build a new power hierarchy. For this reason failed presidential candidates typically disappear from public life. I want to cover the purpose-driven model of effective leadership first because failures in that model can be adjusted for, the vision can remain intact, and the team can move forward even after devastating defeats.

David's Actions

As we walk through the story of David's battle with Goliath, you will see him make his decision to lead. We will notice from his actions that he is aware that every decision he makes supports someone's vision. Though we are not given insight into David's thinking, we can see from his decisions that he understands the precept that all decisions have consequences.

To these three precepts, we will add many more that together form a framework of understanding that defines effective leadership. Yes, some people do these things naturally, as a part of their personality and character. You may be like me, not born to lead, but with diligent attention and circumspection, the application of these precepts will deliver the same results of effective leadership.

In human experience, there is no greater satisfaction to be had than leading a team to build a vision. Consider it—the world changed according to the vision that you, as the leader, put forth and your team worked to achieve. Done correctly, you will create improvements in the world around you. But do not think only good times are ahead, because opposition to your leadership is inevitable. Handle those tough times well, and your team will be behind you, more committed than ever, ready to work out their delegation to hold you up when those stresses return. Teach them to apply the precepts in this book, and you will never be alone in making tough decisions. All you must do to begin is choose to lead.

Precepts

- Choose to lead.
- Every decision supports someone's vision.
- Decisions have consequences.

Email Advice

Mr. Johnson was happy that morning as he pulled his Volvo into his usual spot in front of his Bay Area office. As the production manager, he liked to arrive early and get a good jump on the day. In fact, an hour of basketball at the gym before work had already given him a jump. As he turned on the lights in his office and noticed the stacks of papers and sundry computer parts filling his office, he made a mental note to set aside time at the end of the day for a little housekeeping.

The computer screen came up with the touch of a key, and his email was right on top where he left it yesterday, but with twenty new emails to add to the 130 left over from yesterday. With the speed and agility he had just demonstrated on the court, he attacked the list, starting at the oldest email. *That order is finished. Good. Delete. And that only took five seconds. This will be a productive day! That part is still on backorder. I knew that. Delete. Another five seconds well spent.*

The day did not go as well as expected. Out of the 150 emails, half, seventy-five emails, would require only five seconds to answer, but not all of them will be seen today. Thirty-seven of the emails will take approximately five minutes to handle. Thirty-five of the emails will require a good ten minutes to resolve. Only three emails will take an hour to handle correctly, but Mr. Johnson will get to only one of those today, because all 150 emails will require twelve and a half hours of work, and he never works more than ten hours a day. By lunch, he is in a frenzy of focused email attention and beyond the reach of his team members for communication. At quitting time, a team member asked about vacation time to have surgery and was told to send an email reminder. An hour after his production team has left the building, Mr. Johnson finally notices the stack of fifteen hard drives that had been added to the clutter on the office floor. Though he could not remember at this point why they were there, he was sure someone had sent him an email about it.

Between problems with the WIP inventory, two meetings, and running the office football pool, he got through all but fifty of the emails he started the day with, and only forty new ones had come in. It was a good day. He made progress on the backlog. One of the emails he did not read was from the company president wanting to know why three of the orders were now a week late, and the client had taken his business elsewhere. (Another was an automated reminder that the part was still on backorder, so the lost business was somebody else's problem.) The last was from his most productive team member, and it said, "Bye. I am not coming back here for all the money in the world!" But those were problems to be dealt with the next day.

If the email requires only five seconds to answer, then stop it from coming at all. Those little data points should be plotted in graphs and charts associated with an information system. Here are some simple rules to follow concerning how your email interacts with an information system:

- *Never* set up an automated notification to come from the information system to your email.
- *Never* design a process for your team that includes even one step where you get an email.
- *Never* have reports emailed to you on a schedule, because by the time you look at them, the data is no longer real time. Set up a real-time analytics dashboard in the information system and go there when you need to know.

These are three of the biggest wastes of valuable time ever created by the information age. If it only requires five seconds to deal with, then it is nothing for the leader to handle anyway. That is why you have a team.

The five-minute issues are clerical items that would better be handled by team members, so give them the responsibility and authority they need to handle those clerical issues. Even the ten-minute emails are small issues of individual concern that would amount to baby steps on the path to accomplishing your vision. Delegate those as well. And a truly effective leader will also delegate the three critical emails to key team members for investigation, dissection, discussion, and consensus before they are emailed to you for a five-minute review and approval. Do not forward the emails to your team members; make sure they get them instead of you. Yes, spend only fifteen minutes a day answering emails and the rest on leading your team. Imagine how quickly they will accomplish the vision if they get that much leadership attention. Use email to get pictures from your family and compliments from your boss.

2

---•---

START AT THE
BEGINNING

L eading a team begins at the beginning. That is right; no team to lead, no authority to use, no responsibility to make decisions, nothing for you to be accountable for. The world is familiar, and the day-to-day movements are comfortable. Take a deep breath, because the moment you decide to exercise that first precept, and you choose to lead, this place of serenity will go away. Savor this moment and give it time to wash over you and imprint a lifelong memory. When the road to accomplishing your vision gets tough, you will need this memory to hold on to. Now consider: what about this moment of freedom and serenity is so bad that you want to see it changed? That is the starting place for your vision. Not the change you want to see but the current situation.

Open a mapping application on your phone and try routing yourself to this address: Systrakaffi, Klausturvegur, Kirkjubæjarklaustur, Iceland. The food there looks amazing (no, I have never eaten there, nor even been to Iceland). Chances are that unless you are reading an internationally published version of this book, the mapping software will not be able to provide you with a route. There is nothing wrong with the destination, and I am sure that the food tastes as good as it looks, but from where you are now, you cannot walk there for dinner.

You can get there to enjoy a meal but not without a large team of highly skilled people to provide transportation. Not because of where the restaurant is but because of where you are. The employees of Systrakaffi will be cooking tonight at that location even if you do not walk through the doors. Only if you enlist the support of the right people, in the right order, with the right motivation can you hope to satisfy your hunger. That is how leadership begins. Knowing the destination is only theoretical; until you understand your current place, you will not know what to change or even what needs to be changed. The leader begins by knowing their place, their people, and their purpose.

KNOW YOUR PLACE

You need to know your place. This is not a classist comment designed to keep servants subservient. Remember that every decision you make supports someone's vision. Another way of stating this precept is the leader is a servant to those he follows and those he leads. Servant because the choices you make, if made circumspectly, will not be guided by what you need but by what they need. You can think about dinner at Systrakaffi, but if you try to order it at the airport ticket counter, the team there will be too confused to act.

David knew his place. "And David was the youngest: and the three eldest followed Saul. But David went and returned from Saul to feed his father's sheep at Bethlehem" (1 Samuel 17:15–16).

David followed his father's leadership as a member of the family. He followed King Saul's leadership as a member of the nation of Israel in general, and as a man of age, he also served in the standing army under Saul's authority. David received a full delegation from his father for managing the family's shepherds, and he delegated portions of that authority and responsibility to the servants who comprised his shepherding team. Though David also had a delegation in Saul's army, he was at home, in his place, doing his job, with the sheep. Then David's father wanted to know how his older sons, who were serving in the army, were doing. Jesse also had an obligation under Saul's authority to provide rations for the troops. "And Jesse said unto David his son, Take now for thy brethren an ephah of this parched corn, and these ten loaves, and run to the camp to thy brethren; And carry these ten cheeses unto the captain of their thousand, and look how thy brethren fare, and take their pledge" (1 Samuel 17:17–18).

The phrase that interested me most about this passage is "the captain of their thousand." Israel consisted of twelve tribes, and the standing army was organized around those tribes or family units. David would deliver food to the captain of "their thousand," which distinguishes that captain from any other captains from that same tribe, suggesting at least two such captains from David's tribe. Extrapolate that out; if there were two such captains from each of the twelve tribes, that is an army of 24,000 Israelites serving under Saul's authority.

> Now the Philistines gathered together their armies to battle, and were gathered together at Shochoh, which belongeth to Judah, and pitched between Shochoh and Azekah, in Ephesdammim. And Saul and the men of Israel were gathered together, and pitched by the valley

of Elah, and set the battle in array against the Philistines. And the Philistines stood on a mountain on the one side, and Israel stood on a mountain on the other side: and there was a valley between them. (1 Samuel 17:1–3)

When armies meet on the field of battle but do not engage in a fight, they must be so evenly matched that neither has any confidence of victory. From that, we assume that there were approximately 24,000 Philistines in the valley as well. Imagine a football game where the spectators are the players, and there are 48,000 of them at the event. At night, they tailgate in the parking lot. During the day, they fill the stands and wait for instructions to rush onto the field and attack. Forty-eight thousand men in the valley, and David knew his place within that throng.

And David rose up early in the morning, and left the sheep with a keeper, and took, and went, as Jesse had commanded him; and he came to the trench, as the host was going forth to the fight, and shouted for the battle. For Israel and the Philistines had put the battle in array, army against army. And David left his carriage in the hand of the keeper of the carriage, and ran into the army, and came and saluted his brethren. (1 Samuel 17:20–22)

Notice that he knew that the battle was on when he saw how the army was positioned. He also knew who on his team could receive a delegation, who was the keeper of the carriages, and, in a valley filled with 48,000 men exactly where to find his brothers. David did not start the day as the hero of Israel but as his father's shepherd, his king's subject, and his brothers' subordinate in the army. He never would have gotten to be a hero if he had not first known his place in the authority structure. First, he delegated some of his authority and responsibility to a keeper, assuring the sheep would be tended to in his absence. Second, he dutifully executed his delegation to bring food to the army by knowing who the keeper of the carriages was and where he could be found in the valley. Third, he ran to his brothers and to his proper place within the valley. Each action indicated his understanding of the delegations he had received and of where he fit in the authority structures. He clearly knew his place.

For every leader, this is the starting point, knowing your place. Great opportunities to change the world will come your way, but if you are not there, you will miss them. David knew his place, and he made haste once on the scene to get to it. He served his father by delivering the food. He served his king by getting to his post. Once at his post, he served his brothers by acknowledging their authority; he saluted. Life-changing opportunities will often be passed down to you from those you follow, so make sure they know you are there, ready to act responsibly.

This precept leads to one undeniable truth about life: if you are in your place, then there is going to be a job to do. If you are to be a leader, you should first know how to follow both good and bad leadership. You must be doing your job, in your place, for leadership opportunities to develop. Often, wannabe leaders leave their place to attempt to lead in another area. Leadership never starts from some other place. There, you will find that you are in opposition to the leadership in that place, and they will not easily delegate their authority to someone who has not been following their lead. If you want to lead, stay in your place, and do your job.

KNOW YOUR PEOPLE

Once in your place, get to know your people. You will need to know who you follow and who will follow you. Right now, you may be the lowest person on the team, with the least authority. When the moment comes when your cause can be taken up, you will need other people to make it happen. Those people will have their own motivations and purposes that will determine how you interact with them to make them part of your team. Only if you know who they are can you hope to lead them or follow them correctly.

Opportunity is not something that is guaranteed to come your way from those you are following. The leaders you are following may not have your best interests in mind or may not be interested in sharing authority with anyone. Even in these difficult environments, the circumspect leader can find other motivators that might gain authority, even if given grudgingly; David will show us how in a later chapter. But gaining that authority will be impossible if the leader is not circumspectly aware of the type of people he or she is following.

Knowing your place means understanding where you fit in the authority structure. Knowing your people implies that you know who has authority around you and what you can expect them to do with that authority. David did not just run into the army and leave the provisions unattended. He left his carriage with the person who was responsible for keeping the carriages, the one who had the authority to make decisions about the care of the carriages. If David had not known his people, which included knowing who the keeper of the carriages was and what he could be counted on to do in the exercise of his authority, he would have been unable to reach his brothers. Without the help of the keeper, he would never have made it to the correct place to be ready to lead. He had to know his people to get there.

Knowing your people is best simplified by understanding a person's relationship to authority. The Bible discerns four approaches to authority: wiseman, simpleton, fool, and scorner. The wise are those who submit to proper authority, and, knowing their place, they do their job gladly. Those who do not know their place or who do not understand authority are referred to as simple, and they can be taught. Most often leaders' problems come from the foolish, those who know authority but do not take it seriously. The scorner rejects all authority. Each of these groups reacts differently to authority and requires different motivations.

To lead effectively, you must evaluate each leader you follow and each team member to determine which category best approximates their approach to authority. Failing to understand how each person can be expected to handle authority leads to disaster. For instance, trusting a foolish person to deliver a message is a sure way to ensure the message is either not delivered or is corrupted by a lack of fidelity. "He that sendeth a message by the hand of a fool cutteth off the feet, and drinketh damage" (Proverbs 26:6).

Giving a simple person authority they do not understand will ensure it is not used effectively. Giving a scorner authority over a simple person is likely to produce another scorner. Be circumspect in your evaluations.

I have seen many examples of failed leadership, where modern training in tolerance and acceptance leaves no room for discrimination. From this approach of nonjudgment, a leader delegates to everyone with no regard for the possible consequences. Your success as a leader is completely dependent on how effective your team members are at exercising the delegations you give them. Be circumspect and discern for yourself who is ready for that delegation.

Judge carefully who you follow. All leaders are attempting to create change, which implies a certain discontentedness with the current situation. Most often, this leads people to rebellion or lashing out against authority to draw attention to needed change. A rebel/scorner attempts to force those who have authority to agree with their vision and thus create change. In the US, we uphold this quality of radical activism to create change as a noble right, but rebellion only creates confrontation and strife. Though the book of Proverbs was written after David's time, it does give some good instructions for how to deal with those who rebel against or reject authority. "Cast out the scorner, and contention shall go out; yea, strife and reproach shall cease" (Proverbs 22:10). Following a scorner leads to disaster when they are finally cast out.

Knowing what your team members need from you requires discerning each team member's relationship to authority. For instance, Proverbs 9:8 says, "Reprove not a scorner, lest he hate thee: rebuke a wise man, and he will love thee." Reprove in this context would mean correcting the way a team member is using their delegated authority and responsibility. Attempting to correct the scorner will only make the situation worse. *Rebuke* is a word that implies the expression of sharp criticism. And yet a rebuke of a wise person will bind them more tightly to your vision and you as their leader. Treat the scorner as if they are wise, and you will have a fight on your hands. Treat the wise person as you would a scorner, by ignoring or brushing over their behavior, and you may lose their confidence in your leadership.

The book of Proverbs in particular, and the Bible in general, provides all the insight needed to treat the wise person, the simpleton, the fool, and the scorner appropriately. For the best results, as a judge of a team member's authority relationship, I would recommend a continuous study of these concepts. For now, here is a synopsis of what you will find with some high-level thoughts about how to treat each type:

Wise

- Defined as those who are always increasing knowledge, even from the correction and council of others: Proverbs 1:5, 6:6, 8:33, 9:8, 9:9, 10:8, 10:14, 12:15, 13:1, 13:20, 15:31, 17:10, 18:15, 19:20, 21:11, 22:17, 23:19, 24:5, 25:12, 30:24–31.
- Bring joy to those who know them, and leaders should try to have at least one on every team. Proverbs 10:1, 10:5, 14:35, 23:15, 23:24, 27:11.
- These are clean-cut, all-American types who wear clean clothes, comb their hair, and avoid profanity. Proverbs 3:7, 14:16, 15:24, 20:1, 20:26, 21:22, 24:6, 26:5, 26:12, 28:7, 28:11.

- Speak carefully to the profit of others, bringing understanding and resolution in conflict. Proverbs 10:19, 12:18, 14:3, 15:2, 15:7, 16:14, 16:21, 16:23, 17:28, 29:8, 29:9, 29:11.
- Will become effective leaders and can become great leaders. Proverbs 1:5, 3:35, 11:29, 11:30, 13:14, 14:1, 14:24, 17:2, 21:20.

The wise people you find tend to already be leaders. Showing them a vision that makes sense and obtaining their buy-in is easy. Effective leaders spend most of their organizational, instructional, and developmental time with the wise members of their team because those members provide the most support. Share the load with them and confidently allow them to make decisions. Give them access to information and explain your value system to them; even if they do not personally accept your values as their own, they will make decisions based on your values, except where they conflict with their own.

Simple

- These people can become wise but have not learned their place within the authority structure, or they may not even yet realize that they answer to the authority of others. Proverbs 1:4, 7:7, 8:5, 9:4, 9:13, 9:16, 19:25, 21:11.
- Because they lack wisdom concerning authority, they can be led to destruction or be distracted to make poor decisions with a delegation. Proverbs 1:32, 14:15, 14:18, 22:3, 27:12.
- They enjoy being simple; it suits them. Proverbs 1:22.

Provide consistent and patient instruction to convert the simple into wise people. They are flighty, never staying with one thing for long. Any new idea will fascinate them, but they never develop a full understanding before moving on to something new. They may never have been exposed to the ideas of authority and responsibility. Often their development is arrested in childhood by parents who told them what to do, rather than teaching them to choose wise actions. These team members can be effective and efficient at accomplishing specific assigned tasks but will sit idle after those tasks are complete. Unfortunately, giving them instructions for subsequent action may overwhelm them, so assign one task at a time. Teach them the effective uses of authority before giving small delegations. As they learn to use authority to make decisions, they can be converted into wise people.

Foolish

- Fools take pleasure in ignoring authority whenever they can and will strongly resist wisdom, preferring instead to have fun and make fun of anything serious. Proverbs 12:15, 17:10, 17:16, 18:2, 23:9, 27:22, 28:26, 29:9.
- Will be punished by their own actions. Proverbs 7:22, 10:8, 10:10, 11:29, 26:1, 26:3, 26:10, 26:12, 30:21–22.
- Behave in silly and perverse ways that make no sense. Proverbs 9:13, 10:23, 14:1, 17:24, 19:10, 21:20, 24:7, 26:11.
- Bring suffering and pain into the lives of everyone around them. Proverbs 9:6, 10:1, 10:14, 15:5, 15:20, 17:12, 17:21, 17:25, 19:13, 20:3, 26:4, 26:5, 26:6 (send a message by a fool?), 26:8, 27:3.
- Speech is prideful, perverse, and rough; they cuss often and are fond of telling off-color jokes that make the wise uncomfortable. Proverbs 10:18, 12:16, 13:16, 14:3, 14:7, 14:16, 15:7, 17:7, 17:28, 18:6, 18:7, 19:1, 29:11, 29:20.

The fools on your team are long-term projects. Because they recognize authority, they will perform well under direct supervision. In an area of giftedness or expertise, they can even be left to their own devices, since the pride achieved through performance is sufficient to ensure they make good decisions. Outside of these areas of perfection, they prefer to assert their autonomy and can be counted on to distract the simple from their assigned task. If a scorner is present, they are easily enticed into acts of rebellion that often have disastrous personal consequences. Helping them develop a new area of expertise in leadership is one effective way to encourage them to make some wise decisions, though they will always retain a portion of their silly behavior and prideful bravado.

Scorner

- They are dangerous to deal with and proud of it; beware. Proverbs 9:7, 9:8, 21:24.
- They reject all wisdom and set themselves in opposition to authority. Proverbs 13:1, 14:6, 15:12.
- They are only useful as bad examples, are ready for destruction, and should be removed from your team as quickly as possible. Proverbs 19:25, 22:10, 24:9.

The scorner cannot be converted because they reject proper authority. Unfortunately, these are typically highly gifted individuals who will impress you as potential high achievers. Hatred of authority overrides any good intention they have, even to the point of rendering pride an ineffective motivator. Though they may perform given tasks with exceptional results, they will at the same time engage in subversive behavior that will damage your team and your leadership.

Time reveals their true nature. Scorners hide well. When you are forced to defuse conflict and strife between team members, look to see who is standing just outside of that conflict or bringing the issues to your attention. If the same person is always hanging around those areas of turmoil, then they are causing it. Attempting to correct this behavior will not work and will only produce a worse result. Get rid of the scorner before they set themselves up in open revolt.

Some scorners are hard to see because they have learned the proper language of submission. They can easily profess their undying loyalty to your cause, while at the same time conspiring with the foolish to destroy your leadership. Your success as a leader is dependent on being open to assessing the results of the scorner's actions instead of any justifications they may provide. If you see a consistent pattern of results that indicate opposition to authority (yours or other leaders'), then you must not hesitate to take appropriate action.

Getting rid of the scorner is not always possible. Often, they are on the team because a leader above you in the hierarchy has placed them there. In larger business organizations, you may not be at liberty to dismiss a person immediately without justification. During the time required to assemble proper justification for their removal, the scorner will be aware of the action against them, and they will enter open revolt. Cast them out immediately where possible. If you cannot do so, reduce their delegations to areas where they can function as independent contributors to limit their opportunities to influence the team.

A word of caution about the psychological development of adolescents, who often rebel against parental authority. Continued efforts to reform their approach to authority may yet result in a wise adult. As adolescents, they have not yet fully developed their relationship with authority, and your influence can broaden their options and improve their choices. Consider that part of authority is the ability to see to it that your decisions are carried out. An adolescent is transitioning from their dependent state of existence with no authority into an adult life where they gain authority at least in their own affairs. Experimentation with asserting that authority should be expected and if possible redirected to a full understanding of the hierarchical nature of authority. An adolescent who understands how to take their place within the hierarchy is more likely to be successful in moving up in that hierarchy. Teach them their place rather than attempting to put them in it.

Choose Carefully

If the opportunity exists, take care in choosing team members. Most teams come together because of time and location. Those people were in one location with a communal problem when a leader stepped forward and presented a vision. These teams contain members with each of the four approaches. The scorner will work against the team and make every effort to thwart the vision, even if it is in their own self-interest. Fools will do the work while mocking the vision and wasting time. A simpleton will be excited about the work and lack the ability to make effective decisions but can perform one small task at a time. Only a wise person contributes quality decision-making and can be a leader within the team. Choose only wise people if you can.

Be ready to utilize the people around you when the moment arrives to change the world. The scorner can be assigned to functioning as an individual contributor. Consistently remind the fool to attend to their delegation, but be ready to adjust to their foolishness, while remembering that they will be punished by their actions. Do not attempt to lessen that punishment but adding to it can increase the scorner's influence. The simpletons require constant attention to help them move from one task to the next. As the leader, you are currently responsible for providing that oversight, but that responsibility can be made a part of a delegation to another team member. Delegate oversight of the simple to the wise on your team. All the members of your team can be productive if you understand their relationship with authority.

Judge Privately and Circumspectly

One cautionary note about judging: do not apply these labels openly to those you judge. This categorization of people is often frowned upon by those who want to act foolishly or simply while thinking themselves wise. The scorner will always be in open rebellion but may not be looking for a fight and pointing a finger at them will bring conflict. Knowing your people is a quiet, internal communication that you use to help you act appropriately toward each team member.

People do not fit into boxes easily. These categories are flexible, and you may notice that some people seem to fit in more than one category. While seeing wise behavior from a scorner is not likely, they may submit to authority on a sports team, social organization, or within their gang affiliation. This submission to authority outside your authority will not make them wise on your team. The wise person may overlook your mistakes, but the simpleton and fool will reject your leadership and become scorners. Given the correct instruction, the simpleton can become wise, then decide to act the fool. Be ready to adjust your judgement as they change over time.

Know who is following your leadership. If you are fortunate enough to be allowed to choose your team, seek to fill it with wise people. More than likely, you will be working with a team that you did not choose and moving the fool and the simpleton down the path to acting wise will be as much a part of your leadership as defining the vision for the team. In fact, since the big work will be accomplished by the team and not by the leader, you should spend most of your waking hours focused on moving everyone on your team into the wise category. That movement will only happen if you understand where they are starting from and provide the correct inspiration for change. But never try to reform the scorner; you will find only suffering in that effort.

Be careful with this last. Scorners attempt to convince the foolish and the simple to follow them in rebellion. They are practiced in presenting a lie wrapped in truth to make them convincing. Leaders often see this ability at persuasion as a useful tool to apply as a motivational force to shift the team to a new vision. The scorner is not interested in that vision and will only set out to prove it to be a waste of time. While they may help you motivate the team, their motive is to prove that the team's actions are fruitless. Do not trust the scorner to support you when they see the wisdom behind your vision. They will never look for that wisdom, and your efforts to show it to them will only strengthen their hold on the rest of the team when they see the scorner's unwavering resolve. Do the unpleasant thing and get rid of the scorner before they get rid of you.

KNOW YOUR PURPOSE

Why do you want to do something about the current situation? This is not a simple matter that can be decided and put to rest in a few seconds of discontent. Remember that not all the events that will take place on the path to accomplishing your vision will be pleasant. Some of these unpleasant times may even be dangerous, depending on the nature of your vision. Only with a complete and unwavering commitment to a purpose can a leader hope to remain steadfast through these trials. You will need to know your purpose.

A purpose needs to be bigger than the life of the leader. There will be gains and advantages that the leader is attempting to create for their own life, but your life touches the lives of everyone else on the planet. Circumspectly considering the outcomes for everyone else will help you develop a vision that the whole team will buy into, and those others who are not part of the team but are impacted by its actions will be able to buy in as well. The vision you present to them needs to be rooted in a purpose that is all-encompassing. Consider most stridently the impact your vision will have on those whom you are following, since you may need additional authority from them to accomplish that vision. If they are not fully informed and for their own reasons committed to your vision, you may find yourself hung out to dry as a scapegoat before having time to accomplish your goals.

"What's in it for me?" This is an easy question for you to answer for you. Consider how you will approach discovering this for all those other people. This will take time, and it should not be rushed. If you present an expected outcome to a team member, only to find out it is in opposition to their stated purpose in life, you may lose their support. The easiest way to find out is to ask; do not state. It may seem cliché to ask people where they want to be in five years, but any answer will give insight into what that team member values and wants to accomplish. The leaders you follow, even the bad ones, will usually have clear expectations of your performance. Knowing those expectations helps you develop a comprehensive purpose that will sustain your vision to the end.

This statement of purpose is for you, the leader. You will require a purpose that you have decided is right and appropriate for the direction you want your life to go. Choose a purpose that will get you out of bed before the alarm sounds and get you busy working on it from the moment your feet hit the floor. Choose a purpose that you can remain committed to through years of attempting to acquire the needed authority, or even decades of struggle to accomplish a small portion of the vision. Simple purposes that include only you and your immediate needs will not suffice for long-term success. If your purpose is only to get a 10 percent increase in your pay over the next year, how disappointed would you be if you only got 3 percent after two years of effort?

Think big and broad. Be circumspect and include everyone in your purpose. Then pause … wait … do not commit until you must. Give yourself all the time you need to be sure that failure in the attempt to live this purpose is good enough. If your life ends the day after committing to this purpose, will you see that effort as having been worth it?

Keep it singular. This may seem a contradiction to the previous statement of big and broad, but that is in reference to your thinking. The purpose should be one thing. Only one. A multipurpose will eventually put you in conflict with yourself when you must choose between purposes. Choose now and dedicate yourself to a single purpose. Since you can only accomplish one purpose, be certain that the effort will be worth it.

There may come a time when sharing parts of your purpose with team members will help them to redefine their own purpose, but your purpose is for you and should be kept private. This is your positive motivator that will allow you to remain calm in the face of opposition from the world and from your team. Keep in mind that the fool and the scorner will turn your own purpose against you if they are aware of it. For this reason, be reluctant to share too many details about it. The vision will be a separate part of the plan, and while it will reflect your purpose, it should not be the purpose.

Dedication to a purpose as large as what I have described will not be easy. Over time, important pieces at the edges of your purpose will begin to fade, so write it down and review it regularly. Your purpose may fit on a single page, or it may be a thirty-page manifesto, but if you do not capture the whole thing, you will lose it. Writing it down also helps you commit fully.

What if I got it wrong? You cannot. That does not mean that a year from now you will agree fully with everything that you wrote, or that you will not discover an aspect of your purpose that you were not aware of when you first wrote it. That is OK. As you learn and broaden your understanding, adjust your purpose. Small adjustments should happen but beware of changing your purpose entirely. Your team is committed to a vision based on your original purpose, and a dramatic shift in the leader's purpose can shatter the vision.

After reviewing what you have written, find a single phrase that will remind you of the full contents. For me, it is Ephesians 5:15. You may pick a quote from a favorite author or a famous saying from one of your country's founding fathers or mothers. The phrase should be small and easy to remember. While I would not recommend sharing your full purpose with your team, this phrase can help new members decide quickly who you are and what you care about.

David's full purpose is not written in the Bible, but one phrase could be used to describe that purpose to us. "And when he had removed him, he raised up unto them David to be their king; to whom also he gave their testimony, and said, I have found David the son of Jesse, a man after mine own heart, which shall fulfil all my will" (Acts 13:22). The simple phrase "Man after God's own heart" would tell us what we could expect this man to do according to the purpose he has chosen for his life. Living up to a purpose statement that demanding throughout life may be impossible, but it is worth trying. Write out your purpose, choose a statement, and prepare to see what David will dare to do with his purpose.

GET STARTED

Leading a team to accomplish a vision is a step-by-step process. Try to start in the middle of your trip to Klausturvegur, Kirkjubæjarklaustur, Iceland, and you will freeze before you drown. When you start at the beginning and do the necessary work to define your place, your people, and your purpose, you can choose from the menu tonight. Bring a coat. I hear it is cold in Iceland.

PRECEPTS

- Start at the beginning.
- Know your place.
- Know your people.
- Know your purpose.

3

———◆●◆———

MOTIVE POWER

Y ou cannot lead if no one will follow. In chapter 1, we examined the concept of authority. If the leader received a proper delegation of authority and responsibility, the team would naturally be on board, right? Try walking into a room occupied by ten to fifteen people you do not know, who have been working together for the last few years and announcing that you are in charge because you were hired as the manager. Even the threat of violence, "Do your job, or I will fire you," is not likely to provide much traction. None of the people you need on your team will follow without some motivation. The next precept we find is that making a change consistent with your purpose requires motivating a team. Or more succinctly, change requires motive power.

Motive power is the energy used to drive machinery. Like the locomotive of the rail lines or the tractor-trailer of the roads, a leader needs motive power to move the team. Changing the view from the front window of a big rig requires motion. Turn the steering wheel left and right all you want, but if you are not moving, the view is not changing. Your team will be the same way. They must move to create any change. Change requires motive power.

Each of us is an independent actor, with free will to do as we like. Why do we seek out the company of other free actors and band together for a common cause? Economic theory has tried to explain this for generations by declaring that we act in our own self-interest, joining others in common cause for mutual benefit. In my experience, people seldom act independently and in common cause unless they follow a leader. Leaders are required to supply the motive power to unite individuals in common cause.

Motive power moves machines. Motivation moves people. Motivation is the idea not yet realized that causes someone to act. Focus on the fact that ideas happen in the mind. Motivation is shaping or growing an idea in the mind of another person. This is not a part of a leader's role that can be done casually, and it requires a patient commitment to persevere in your efforts. The easiest course of action is to find an idea that is already in the team member's mind and tie the needed action to it. If you cannot find an idea to work with, consider finding a new team member, because trying to insert a new idea is a daunting task.

Motivation is either positive or negative, meaning the actor is either trying to see the idea realized or to avoid it. This idea could be the monetary reward to be had, the fun and excitement to be created, the respect of peers, the admiration of the leader, or the destruction that would follow failing to act. Our world was created to operate on the principle of cause and effect. The desire to realize or avoid the idea causes the actions, which are the effects. As stated in most psychology textbooks, we move toward pleasure and away from pain. Neither pleasure nor pain needs to exist; they can be unrealized ideas.

Please do not confuse this discussion about change requiring motive power with the discussion on knowing your people. Knowing your people requires judging which response-to-authority category they are in. Motivating requires knowing what idea they are pursuing, but you do not need to decide if you approve or disapprove of that idea. People act according to some simple patterns that can be observed, defined, and predicted, but people are not pieces on a chessboard. Occasionally, the fool will act in ways that are not in their own self-interest. Motivating a fool to act according to the team's needs is no different from motivating the wise person. Your job as the leader is not to judge the validity or propriety of the idea but simply to use it to motivate action.

You might be thinking that this sounds a little like manipulation instead of motivation. The difference depends on how well you know your team members. The leader needs to know not just who they are but also who they are trying to become. Getting each person to perform their role on the team reliably requires a delegation and motivation that is consistent with each team member's self-image. Choosing a different image for them and attempting to motivate them to become what you have chosen is manipulation.

Manipulation is attempting to use an unrealized idea to cause actions that are inconsistent with the motivated person's chosen self-image. Treat a team member this way, and watch their performance degrade daily. Motivation creates actions that are consistent with the team member's self-image, and for best results, that action will be in the best interests of the team. Manipulation only destroys the team member. As the leader, you do not get to choose and mold your ideal version of a team member; you can only help them realize their chosen ideal. Assisting them to create their ideal image of themselves is motivation.

Regardless of someone's approach to authority, or their conformance to their ideal self-image, we can all be motivated with an unrealized idea. Though this may seem complicated, we have only three built-in motivations and one we may learn as we mature. Examined closely, all motivations will fit into one of these four categories: pleasure, possession, pride, or purpose. Motivating a team member requires knowing which of these will create the strongest idea for a given team member and then showing them how to realize that idea by taking the proper action. Properly motivated team members act reliably and independently, making decisions and taking actions consistent with the accomplishment of the vision, because that action is also consistent with their self-image.

Pleasure

Pleasure is any physical sensation that causes us to feel happy. It could be as simple as getting a hug from a loved one or as complex as the dopamine rush experienced by runners after miles of foot-pounding abuse. Repeated exposures to most pleasures create patterns of behavior that bring us back for more. This motivator can lead to addiction, so exercise care when using pleasure as a motivator.

The dark side of pleasure seeking is its antithesis—the avoidance of pain. The pain could be physical or psychological. Past experiences have created an association between a type of action and a negative or painful result. Fear of the return of that pain motivates the team member to avoid those actions. Because fear can be such an effective short-term motivator, this desire to avoid the idea of pain can easily override other positive motivators you may have put in place. For that reason, using fear deliberately as a motivator is always counterproductive.

Helping a team member remove fear as a motivator is a better option. Removing fear is never easy, but the steps are simple. As a one-on-one coaching moment, convince the person to perform the action with you as a safety net, to prevent the pain. Then ensure that the result is pleasure instead of pain. Usually, this involves a lot of over-the-top praise and then celebration when the action is completed. Grossly exaggerate your praise. The team member should see your celebration as an unusual, almost strange response that brings an awkward uncontrollable smile and giggle. If they are not blushing, you are not far enough over the top. You are trying to overcome fear, so pull out all the stops. Do not expect this to be a one-time coaching moment; you will need to repeat this frequently.

Frustration over the need to repeat often is your enemy in the correction process. Demonstrating frustration at the need to repeat replaces the former fear with a new one. Instead of the fear of making a random person angry, for example, the team member now fears disappointing the leader. That new fear produces activity that is useful for the team in the short term, but what happens when the team member stops being afraid? This could even be a positive turning point in their development, where they have finally replaced fear with a positive motivator, with the leader's help. But now their opinion of the leader, who has kept them in fear for so long, diminishes. While working with a team member to remove a negative pain motivator, smiles, kind words, and calm assurance are needed.

When frustration about repetition sets in, focus on the pattern of actions you are attempting to create in the team member. We tend to see motivation as a finite series; after pushing the button x times, the team member can be counted on to perform. People are not that predictable. You also have an unrealized ideal self-image. You can sympathize with the team member's difficulties. If you struggle with achieving that ideal image, expect the same from your team members. Sympathy keeps a lid on frustration over the need to repeat.

Sympathetic repetition can help break through resistance. Unless you are fortunate enough to find an extant idea, team members will resist your efforts at motivation. Be ready for resistance and allow yourself to not respond to it. Persevere in your efforts to be convincing if you know the motivational idea will create actions consistent with the team member's image of their ideal self. Avoid arguing about it at all costs. Arguing is not consistent with sympathy, and your insistence will be seen as an intrusion into the team member's relationship with their ideal self. The objective is not to prove you are right. The objective is to motivate.

Simple pleasures are easy motivators to apply. To start the motivational process, begin with some of these simple pleasure ideas that work surprisingly well for short-term gains on everyone.

- Everyone enjoys eating, so the simple promise of a pizza if a short-term goal is achieved can be a surprisingly effective motivator.
- A handshake along with a compliment of a job well done (no hugs since these can be misinterpreted).
- Bring a cake to celebrate a small victory—chocolate, sugar, and a reinforcing of the desire to accomplish goals.
- The most universal pleasure motivator is laughter. Try to avoid sarcasm or laughter directed at a team member. Simple humor that gets everyone teary-eyed is a great motivator. No off-color humor because it appeals to a different aspect of pleasure.
- If you want to help mold a team member's motivational idea, try having a regular cadence of meetings over coffee. Studies have shown that caffeine increases a person's willingness to say yes and accept new ideas (https://www.abc.net.au/science/articles/2006/05/01/1627382.htm).

If discovering a pleasure to motivate a team member proves difficult, then pleasure may not be a strong enough idea for this person. To be certain, try being direct and ask, "What makes you happy?" Failing with the direct approach, try other motivators. Pleasure is the weakest of the three primary motivators anyway, because of the rinse and repeat nature. Repetition does have the advantage of continual reinforcement, which can produce long-term results, especially when removing an avoidance of pain motivation.

Possession

We spend the largest part of our day focusing on what we want or need. The order of want then need is significant. While this may not be true in most of the world, in the United States, our needs are well met, freeing us to be intensely focused on our wants. Stress and tension that once pushed us into survival mode to find food for the family now focus on the accumulation of stuff.

Mr. Bannerman was not satisfied with Allen's performance. After a year of constant attempts to motivate him to get serious about selling more appliances, this month's sales figures were falling. With nothing left to lose, Mr. Bannerman asked Allen what he really wanted in life. The response was immediate. Allen took out of his wallet a catalog photo of the Rolex watch he wanted to wear. And without hesitation, Mr. Bannerman tripled Allen's goal for the next month and promised to get him the Rolex if he hit the new goal. Had Allen stopped to think it through, he would have realized that the cost of the Rolex would not be offset by less than ten times that number of sales, but the desire to possess the watch overrode his internal value calculations, and he went to work feverishly to hit the goal.

Three weeks later (ahead of schedule), with a victorious flourish, Allen entered Mr. Bannerman's office with the final bill of sale to hit his goal. Mr. Bannerman celebrated this last sale loudly throughout the office, before grabbing his keys and shoving Allen into the front seat of his car. They drove downtown to the jeweler, and Mr. Bannerman made a generous 10 percent down payment on the watch. Mr. Bannerman handed the watch to the wide-eyed Allen along with the payment book and told him to keep up the excellent work and the payments.

Do not worry. Allen did continue to work at the expected pace. Fifteen years later when he told me this story, it was obviously a good memory for him. He still wore the watch then. Over the years, Mr. Bannerman became more of a father figure to Allen than a motivational sales manager, and they had a lifelong relationship that I was fortunate enough to witness. The love, devotion, and respect that Allen displayed toward Mr. Bannerman were moving.

The possession motivator can backfire, often with cataclysmic results. Consider the irrational people who get arrested on Black Friday morning, shoving people out of their way to buy a TV at half price. The desire to possess taps into those deep areas of our brain where failure is not an option. Ownership becomes a matter of survival. When using a possession motivator, the leader is promising that the object of desire can be had. There will be a crashing moment if the leader cannot deliver. Maybe the funding needed for an increase in salary was not possible. More commonly, the increase in pay is achieved, but the team member spends the increase on a different set of wants. The desire to possess that unrealized idea of a specific want will override the recognition of cause and effect, leaving the leader at fault for the perceived loss.

The most common misstep with the possession motivator is forgetting that the team member misvalued the object of desire. Mr. Bannerman knew the value of the watch and knew the sales quota would not be an offset. Allen believed that possessing the watch was worth any price. His valuation of the watch led him to work harder than ever before, using all the hunter-gatherer skills that once fed the family. Nothing mattered except having the watch. Even though it was not a fully realized possession when he received it, he became bound to the leader who put it in his hands.

Allen did tell me he was mad at first, but every time he looked at the watch on his arm, he was grateful to Mr. Bannerman for giving it to him. In Allen's case, gratitude was enough to get him to reset his valuation. Over time, he understood that the watch should have been a long-term goal, realized after many years of careful planning and execution. For Allen, the value of the watch far exceeded its cost. The results of his changed work habits meant that throughout his life, he could easily have purchased hundreds of such watches, but he only needed that one. He gladly spent the next three years making the payments on the watch, but not everyone will respond this way.

All salespeople like Allen eventually deal with buyer's remorse. After getting the desired object, the buyer is now able to clearly see its real value. Freed from the hunter-gatherer mental state, the object is revalued and often falls short of the cost. The immediate outcome is a desire to return the object and blame the salesperson who convinced them to buy it. Leaders who find themselves in the role of the salesperson, in this case, are in big trouble and will lose the team member.

Annual review time in an organization can be very trying for a leader because of buyer's remorse. A team member who has diligently applied themselves to improving last year's review has been using the idea of a raise as a motivation. When that idea is realized, motivation disappears, and revaluation can take place. Small increases in pay rarely improve a team member's financial picture significantly. If the revalue of the raise does not offset the effort to achieve it, the team member will blame the leader (as the salesperson) and will leave the team shortly after getting the raise.

Buyer's remorse is the most common pitfall, but a satisfying revaluation can be just as demotivating. With the object in hand and the idea fully realized, the team member simply fades away. In a temporary state of satisfaction, they lose their motivation because they have no unrealized idea. Immediate action from the leader to help the team member find a new object of desire or other motivator is the only way to prevent this team member from leaving. Sometimes they leave before the leader even knows they are gone. A patient leader will leave the door open for their return, since a new object will soon replace the old one. If this team member delivered quality results while motivated, they will do so again.

As you can see, being circumspect in using the possession motivator is necessary. Only in rare cases like Allen's will the realization of the possession idea produce the desired result. Most team members who get their objects of desire will leave the team shortly afterward. Only a leader who sees the fulfillment coming and prepares another idea in advance will have much hope of keeping them. Preplanning is the only safeguard.

Another mistake often made when using possession motivators is substitution. Consider how disappointed Allen would have been had Mr. Bannerman purchased an Apple watch instead of the Rolex. Arguing with Allen about the relative lack of functionality of the Rolex compared to the app-heavy Apple watch would not have changed Allen's mind about owning the Rolex. Allen's fight-or-flight response would have been triggered, and he would have stormed out of the jeweler's, never to return. A new apartment, when a house is the idea, a Toyota instead of Mercedes, chicken instead of steak, or Rolex instead of Timex, the idea will be specific, and only the right possession will satisfy.

Some possession ideas can become unhealthy motivators. Unhealthy motivational relationships cannot be changed and are impossible to fulfil. These obsessions are unhealthy because the lack of proper valuation has led a team member to choose an object that will remain far out of reach. When using a possession motivational strategy, remember that you possess the right mind to assess value. If you discover an unhealthy idea in a team member, *do not* share your valuation with the team member. The argument that will ensue is counterproductive and unavoidable. Yes, I did this once, and the consequences were unpleasant. Applaud the team member for having an idea of what they want, and never mention that object again. Find another motivator.

Pride

We all want to feel good about who we are. Pride can participate as part of an idea that is driving a pleasure or possession motivator. Wearing a Rolex, for example, declares for all to see that there is something special about the person wearing it. Even the realization that everyone knows that I am the life of any party can be a source of pride. Feeling good about our person, place, or possessions motivates us to extremes of action. Those extremes may benefit the team, but there are some pitfalls to avoid.

The estimation of what makes us feel pride is different for everyone and tied to the ideal self-image. Pride comes from living according to the image. Holding the desired position or title, working for the right company, or even living in the right neighborhood can build pride. Allen's pride grew by putting the right watch on. The temptation when using a pride motivator is to attempt to motivate according to our own ideal self-image. Trying to convert team members to be like you ensures destruction as a leader. To use pride as a motivator, a leader must work with each team member's unique self-image.

Person

Some people gain pride from being a nice person, but others have high demands of performance. Either of these can drive actions that are good for the team, but this pride of person is the most deeply felt and difficult to predict. This is the one area of pride where failure is not an option if a team member is going to be productive.

When using pride-of-person as a motivator, remember that failure is not an option. For this reason, these ideas can be difficult to predict or control. If you miss a deliberate attempt by a team member to demonstrate their best quality and do not deliver the expected praise, this will seem to them a failure on their part. Also, negative events in other parts of a team member's life can produce a failure state that the leader has no control over. Team members who find themselves in a state of failure act in their own self-interest, not in the best interest of the team, and use their delegation for the critical task of restoring their pride.

Place

Pride of place is a little less volatile but also has a complication. The place could be a position within the authority structure, a physical place to live or work, or even a place on an imagined esteem hierarchy of the team. To use this pride as a motivator, ask the team member where they want to be, and if possible, put them there. Sometimes this is as simple as providing a title. Handing out empty titles will backfire. With the title must come a clearly new delegation that is announced to the team, or buyer's remorse will create a boomerang effect. Giving a team member the desk near the door may be a simple rearrangement of furniture but have a massive impact on their performance. Even an announcement to the team of the valuable contributions made recently by this team member can improve their pride of place.

Complications arise when competition begins. Pride of place can be a surprisingly potent source for competition within the team. If anyone feels slighted or demeaned in any way, their immediate response will be to lash out at anyone perceived to be in a better place. Now the desk by the door is a source of contention, another team member's promotion a reminder of failure, and someone else's accomplishments a source of jealousy. Using pride of place as a motivation will require a constant balancing act. Like the plate spinner at the circus, it is only a matter of time before a plate falls.

Possessions

Using pride of possessions as a motivator is almost impossible. The use of the possession motivator does depend somewhat on this pride motivator, but to use the pride itself as a motivator requires that we first predict the outcome of the moment of realization of the possession idea. Since buyer's remorse often changes the valuation, predicting the pride component is unstable at best.

One sailor I knew wanted an IROC Z28, and that was all he ever talked about. He would light up and beam with pride as he described repeatedly what it would be like cruising his hometown in this iconic muscle car. Recruiters and officers had been using this pride of ownership for years to ensure his continued reenlistment. Finally, he had the funds, found the car, and went home on leave to show it off. None of the people he knew ten years ago were still in his hometown cruising the streets on Friday night. And the new crowd did not care about his vintage Z28 with the faded paint job. He went AWOL and never returned to his duty station.

All pride motivators inspire team members to work past obstacles, against impossible odds, to deliver the result. Picture the team member on a tightrope, with obstacles in the way of reaching the other side. Reaching the other side brings applause and typically positive results for the team. But consider the risks.

Use Sparingly

Ask around to discover what makes people proud of who they are: I am a nice person, I am smart, I am strong, I am musical, I am a hard worker, I am always right, and so on. These statements declare a quality that the team member sees as a strength in their life compared to others. This comparative analysis functions well because we can always find plenty of people who are not as smart, strong, or musical. The pitfall is that we only need to find one person whom we consider better in this area to become jealous. If the team member loses confidence in their "I am" statement, their decisions will focus on the restoration of pride, not on the needs of the team. And if another team member is responsible for the loss of confidence, the battle is likely to rip the team apart.

For these reasons, allow pride to be a personal motivator, but limit use of this motivator with your team. Watch for signs of imbalance: furrowed brows, sharp responses, overly insistent arguments, even assertive "I am" statements. Carefully, with calm reasoning, try to adjust the picture to improve the team member's sense of pride. If the center of their pride idea is person, pay them a sincere compliment. Maybe that team member needs to take a lead role in the next team meeting, to improve their pride of place. Or in the case of pride of possessions, ask a question about their most prized possession, even if it is still an unrealized idea. Even this limited involvement with pride motivators is unpredictable, unreliable, and even occasionally disastrous.

THE CAUSE

When David arrived in the valley of Elah, the army was moving into position for the battle. This pattern of behavior was motivated by fear. Saul no longer had the power of God in his life and had stopped leading his army. Now the army geared up and went to their posts, ready for battle, because they were afraid of the consequences if they did not. But they did not attack, because their leader was afraid of the consequences if they did. The whole army feared Goliath and each member of the army was afraid enough that they ran away if Goliath approached them. An army of 24,000 men, whose leader was almost eight feet tall and had been a warrior his whole life, and all were afraid of one man. This is what David found when he arrived.

And he stood and cried unto the armies of Israel, and said unto them, Why are ye come out to set your battle in array? am not I a Philistine, and ye servants to Saul? choose you a man for you, and let him come down to me. If he be able to fight with me, and to kill me, then will we be your servants: but if I prevail against him, and kill him, then shall ye be our servants, and serve us. And the Philistine said, I defy the armies of Israel this day; give me a man, that we may fight together. When Saul and all Israel heard those words of the Philistine, they were dismayed, and greatly afraid. (1 Samuel 17:8–11)

And the Philistine drew near morning and evening, and presented himself forty days. (1 Samuel 17:16)

And David left his carriage in the hand of the keeper of the carriage, and ran into the army, and came and saluted his brethren. And as he talked with them, behold, there came up the champion, the Philistine of Gath, Goliath by name, out of the armies of the Philistines, and spake according to the same words: and David heard them. And all the men of Israel, when they saw the man, fled from him and were sore afraid. And the men of Israel said, Have ye seen this man that is come up? surely to defy Israel is he come up: and it shall be, that the man who killeth him, the king will enrich him with great riches, and will give him his daughter, and make his father's house free in Israel. And David spake to the men that stood by him, saying, What shall be done to the man that killeth this Philistine, and taketh away the reproach from Israel? for who is this uncircumcised Philistine, that he should defy the armies of the living God? And the people answered him after this manner, saying, So shall it be done to the man that killeth him. (1 Samuel 17:22–25)

Motivation that is derived from our inborn drives is difficult to manage and maintain. Saul has given up his role as team motivator, and Goliath has stepped in. Goliath has no desire to see team Israel succeed, so the use of negative motivators is his quickest path to stopping them. His threat of violence, backed by his imposing size, is enough for him to stand off an army.

Goliath lies to create the foundation of his fear motivator. He lies by implying that the only solution to break the stalemate of the two armies is for one man to come down and fight him. A group of one hundred could have rushed out and killed him the first time he suggested it, or the army could just attack. Both would have ended the stalemate. Typically, a fear motivator will have a subtle lie as its foundation. If the lie is penetrated, the fear is removed, and motivation stops, which is why fear is such a short-term motivator.

Notice in verse 25 the list of motivational ideas that the men of Israel have been given as incentives to motivate them to fight Goliath. "The king will enrich him" (1 Samuel 17:25), a possession motivator. Followed by a pleasure motivator, "and will give him his daughter" (1 Samuel 17:25). Wrapped up in a pride of place idea, "and make his father's house free in Israel" (1 Samuel 17:25).

So why did none of these motivational ideas work? Simple. You can lead a team into battle but motivating them to fight on your behalf in single combat against a giant requires something more than an inborn motivator. Saul, as the leader, is surprisingly absent from the battlefield. We are not even told if Saul sent these motivators of money, marriage, and freedom to the front lines. Without a leader providing an overwhelming motivator, only a self-motivated champion will be able to break the stalemate of fear.

Organizing a team and motivating them through the primary motivators is exhausting work. Even if you can make them aware of their own priority motivator and teach them to be self-motivated, they do not always stay on target with the team's objectives. The strength of these motivators is based on an inflated valuation of the unrealized idea. Because the inborn survival instincts eventually get involved with realizing the idea, the idea becomes more important than the goals of the team.

In Saul's name, the ultimate realization of all three ideas was presented to his army, hoping that one of them would become so obsessed that they would act, but since the death of the actor was the most likely outcome, no one was interested. We have all heard stories of men in battle who fell on a grenade to protect their team, but try ordering someone to do so, and the fight might turn against you. Even with excessively valuable motivational ideas to realize, self-preservation may prevail.

David saw Goliath and heard his taunts as well, but his perspective of this imposing enemy was a little different. Fear most often results from the same type of misevaluation that produces buyer's remorse. When a proper valuation is made of the object of fear, the lie is exposed, and typically fear melts away. For David, Goliath was a blasphemer who was defying the army of God. Since God has power over His creation and abhors blasphemy, David knew there was nothing to fear in Goliath's size.

When David speaks up and asks, "Who is this uncircumcised Philistine" (1 Samuel 17:26), he is delivering a new unrealized idea into the motivational mix. This idea speaks not to the weak inborn motivators but to the deeper purpose. David knows his purpose. Because David's purpose is so clearly defined in his thinking, it has become the primary motivator in his life, and he is now able to project it confidently into other people's lives.

His purpose has become so entwined with his life that he can expand it into a cause. Getting even random people to line up behind a cause is almost effortless. Most people never sit down and define their purpose in life. Their actions are motivated by the three inborn motivators and by whatever ill-defined objective the leader of the moment has chosen. Present them with a clearly defined cause, "taketh away this reproach from Israel" (1 Samuel 17:26), and even entrenched fear can be overcome. The key to preparing and delivering a cause is having that well-defined purpose. The problem that needs to be changed, seen in the light of a well-defined purpose, creates a cause that can be shared with the team and become the focus of their motivation.

To see how powerful a cause can be, consider the Loch Ness monster. Some government officials in England raised a question in Parliament in the 1980s about the safety of the Loch Ness monster. Some feared that there would be nothing to prevent poachers and trophy hunters from killing it if Nessie were to surface. In 1985, the British ambassador to Sweden sent a letter to the British parliament asking that they provide some guidance to the Riksdag regarding their concerns to provide legal protection for Storsjöodjuret, a similar mythical creature reportedly living in lake Storsjön. No debate was held, but a letter was returned to Sweden pointing to the British Endangered Species Act as ample projection for any newly discovered creatures.

Discussing the safety of monsters that no one can prove to exist took, at least for a few moments, precedence over the debates on the failing economy, the fall of communism, the rise of terrorism, and the effects of rock and roll on the country's youth. Though I never discovered a specific person as the source for the cause, the exchange of letters demonstrates the power of a cause. With a properly defined and tightly held purpose statement, anyone can create a cause and rally others to participate in realizing that idea. Even to the point of having the governments of two nations discuss how best to protect mythical water monsters.

Purpose

David's purpose became a cause with a simple statement, "taketh away this reproach from Israel" (1 Samuel 17:26). Getting the army to follow him in this cause required a bit more effort. This is the place where most leaders fail because of the harsh resistance they are about to encounter. Getting everyone on board to fight for the cause will tax the leader's strength and test their commitment to their purpose. If you have not actually written down your purpose at this point, stop reading and get that done, or you will not likely make it much further.

Admittedly, this was the one area where I struggled in my early attempts to lead people. I could assemble the logic behind a cause and present it to the team easily enough. But all new ideas when introduced will be rejected. Since I had not written down and fully committed to my purpose, I lacked the strength to persist to see the causes taken up. That commitment is what allows the leader to speak with confidence and assurance of success to repeat the mantra of the cause long enough to see it accepted by the team. Only a clearly defined purpose will sustain.

All new ideas when introduced are rejected. The motivational idea of a cause will be no exception. Only a well-defined purpose will sustain the leader in the coming attack. We find another precept here, that a cause will be opposed.

Resistance

David faced some aggressive resistance to his cause, and it came from his family. David has demonstrated that he knows his place, which would include knowing his place within the family. Culturally, his eldest brother had delegated authority from their father, Jesse, to act as a family leader. Not only did his brother have family authority, but they were in the army, where his elder brother would be his superior officer. So, the resistance David faced came from above him in two authority structures.

And David spake to the men that stood by him, saying, What shall be done to the man that killeth this Philistine, and taketh away the reproach from Israel? for who is this uncircumcised Philistine, that he should defy the armies of the living God? And the people answered him after this manner, saying, So shall it be done to the man that killeth him. And Eliab his eldest brother heard when he spake unto the men; and Eliab's anger was kindled against David, and he said, Why camest thou down hither? and with whom hast thou left those few sheep in the wilderness? I know thy pride, and the naughtiness of thine heart; for thou art come down that thou mightest see the battle. And David said, What have I now done? Is there not a cause? (1 Samuel 17:26–29)

Eliab, David's immediate leader, responded to his cause announcement first with anger. You will get the same reaction if you have chosen a cause that is backed by a purpose that is larger than the needs of the immediate crisis. When leadership becomes ineffective, the crisis of the moment becomes the sole focus. Eliab has no clear guidance from above and a group of fighters looking to him for motivation. He should be taking action to take out Goliath, but without orders to do so and an apparent lack of a purpose, he is frozen by inaction. He is a leader without a proper delegation. He has responsibility but no authority.

When David arrived on the scene, Eliab had already been struggling with his impotence as a leader for forty days, twice a day reminded by Goliath's taunts. His anger demonstrates how powerfully an overvalued pride motivator can backfire. If Eliab's motivations were the same as David's, he would gladly have heard from any member of his team who had an idea. He does not act in the best interest of Israel. He acts harshly and aggressively to restore his pride of place as the leader of this group.

When you set out to create a cause, expect this resistance to your efforts. You may have chosen your leaders wisely, but in every authority structure, there are roadblocks, leaders who have taken pride of place as their primary motivator. They hoard their authority, fearing that if it is delegated, any subordinate can displace them. For David, the leader is his immediate superior. You may face the anger and wrath of someone several levels up the authority chain. Regardless of the authority level, the attack will follow some predictable patterns that you can prepare for.

Wrath

Anger is Eliab's only perceived response. His pride of place has been challenged twice a day for forty days by Goliath. David only draws attention to Eliab's lack of response to the problem of Goliath. Anger is predictable, and so is the pattern of the attack it fuels.

First, anger drives Eliab to question David's right to be there, "Why camest thou down hither?" (1 Samuel 17:28). Pride of place is Eliab's motivator, and he assumes that this is the same for everyone else. His first comment is designed to put David in his subordinate role, to prevent him from using pride of place as a motivation to continue in his questioning. When you attempt to introduce a cause, knowing your place is critical to overcoming this initial attack. If you are out of your place, this angry challenge will be enough to stop your progress. Know that you are in your place, with a cause that is driven by your purpose, and the attack will be ineffective.

The second attack will be even more difficult to hold up against because it is directed at your integrity. Eliab's anger wants to discredit the usurper before he can gain a following. So, he asks, "And with whom hast thou left those few sheep in the wilderness?" (1 Samuel 17:28). He diminishes David's primary role as his father's head shepherd and accuses David of being derelict in filling that role. David's purpose is bigger than taking care of sheep, but because of that purpose, he is always in his place doing the work of seeing the sheep cared for. Before coming to the battlefield, David delegated his shepherd's duties to a keeper. So, while the accusation may have stung a bit, David knows there is no credence. Be in your place doing the work, with a cause that is bigger than the work itself, and this attack can be brushed aside.

Finally, Eliab's anger drives him to attack David's intentions, "I know thy pride, and the naughtiness of thine heart; for thou art come down that thou mightest see the battle" (1 Samuel 17:28). He accuses David of having pride as a primary motivator but then casts that pride as something that is dark and inappropriate. It is at this moment that the attacker reveals his true nature. Eliab only accuses David of what he himself is guilty of. Leaders who use pride of place as a primary motivator will eventually become paranoid, expecting that at any moment their darkest reasoning will be revealed. Because the worst possible outcome for the attacking leader would be to have their deepest fear exposed, they will attempt to use their worst fear to demotivate the object of their wrath. Anger has driven Eliab to give David a weapon that could be used to cripple Eliab—his biggest fear.

Refocus

Three predictable attacks reveal the weakness of the failed leader. Now is the critical moment. David's response to his brother will be crucial in establishing his cause. If he attacks back using the weakness that Eliab has just exposed in himself, his brother will never follow his lead in support of the cause. Those who follow Eliab will resent the successful attack against their leader and reject David's cause. Even if David is not immediately rejected, part of the authority he will need to proceed is being delegated to him through the structure of the army, and it comes to David through Eliab. Any discredit David casts on Eliab will undermine the authority required to move the cause forward. Because of his clear purpose and the immediate need for the cause, David does not answer Eliab's attacks.

This also was a weakness in my early attempts at leadership. Having just been brutally attacked, my first response was always to defend my own pride motivator. And because my opponent had just revealed his weak spot, that was where I would strike back. These attacks were highly effective in crushing my enemy, but they never advanced my cause. Worse, the leader whose support and delegation I might need has lost their pride and will now make no good decisions for the team, but rather, work to restore their pride of place. This last led to me being ejected from the team, so I would not recommend this frontal assault.

Failure to get my causes introduced forced me to focus on this crucial moment. If I knew my place, was in my place doing the work, and had a purpose larger than my own pride, then the attacks would be completely unjustified. The attacks fall under the category of unjust criticism, or more directly lies. While it may seem counterintuitive, not responding is the best course. This demonstrates another precept: defend your cause, not yourself.

David does respond to Eliab but only refocuses attention back to his cause, "And David said, What have I now done? Is there not a cause?" (1 Samuel 17:29). Instead of lashing out to prove that he belonged at the front, because his father sent him. Instead of claiming his pride of place for being the lead shepherd. And without any trace of anger or sarcasm, David points everyone back at Goliath. And Eliab's resistance melts away.

David is now able to step past Eliab and begin speaking to anyone who would hear about his cause. Eventually, his questions about the cause to remove the reproach reach Saul, who sends for him. A cause that is created from a well-defined purpose will require the highest level of authority to pursue. David simply continues to ask questions and points everyone toward the need to remove the reproach of Goliath's blasphemy. As more people begin to see the rightness of the cause, it advances forward.

And David said, What have I now done? Is there not a cause? And he turned from him toward another, and spake after the same manner: and the people answered him again after the former manner. And when the words were heard which David spake, they rehearsed them before Saul: and he sent for him. (1 Samuel 17:29–31)

First Battle Won

Succeeding at gathering a team to rally to a cause will require authority that the leader does not currently have. If you already have the authority, your purpose is too small. The person who wanted to protect the water monsters rallied two governments to exchange information but could not protect either monster on their own. Imagine trying to pull a Nessie militia together by cruising the local taverns and asking for support. Only the top-level authority could make any difference in this cause, and someone had the large, tightly defined purpose that held the cause together long enough to at least get the question asked of Parliament. David needs the king's express authority delegated to him if the reproach is to be removed. David's tightly defined, deeply held purpose allowed him to create a cause and promote it until the king became interested. Now David had to get the delegation he needed to act.

Precepts

- Change requires motive power.
- Motivate with a cause.
- A cause will be opposed.
- Defend your cause, not yourself.

4

———— ◉ ————

KING'S AUTHORITY

I can feel like being called to the principal's office. After keeping your cool while under attack and defending your cause before the people who might comprise your team, now you have been summoned by the boss/CEO/president/pastor/mayor/general, the leader at the top of your local authority structure. You have to share your cause with the king. While you were getting to know your people, hopefully you included the king, because causes need the king's authority.

Kings typically have the power to deal harshly with insubordinate followers. Focusing on that fact will have you dwelling on all the times when you may not have performed perfectly, and fear will cause you to defend yourself instead of your cause. But you are not being called to talk about failures. Stay calm and give the king the same opportunity to hear about your cause as you have given the people.

Know your purpose, because only your purpose should be your motivation at this moment. Though it may be tempting to take this opportunity to see if the king can help with some of your other unrealized ideas, those motivators are not relevant to this meeting. The king wants to hear about the cause you have taken up, to decide if he is ready to participate by giving you a delegation. The hardest motivator to turn off at this moment is pride. Esteem the king for the authority he holds, and not because your pride of place is inflated by being in his presence. Hold on to your purpose tightly.

Preparation trumps reaction. Prepare in those early moments of your leadership while you contemplate the simplicity of your life and decide what needs to change and choose to lead. The easiest way to prepare is to take every opportunity to be in the king's presence. Imagine entering a courtroom for the first time, and in the first five minutes, the judge asks you a question. What happens to your ability to speak? But an attorney who speaks to judges daily articulates an answer with ease.

Even in these encounters, be careful of pride. Get invited to the conference calls the king is attending but avoid speaking. Find out if he is attending any charity events or if your social calendars can overlap at any point but observe the king only; do not seek to engage him. Study his career to be familiar with how he has obtained his delegation. Do not stalk the king. Your objective is not to solicitously engage the king in conversation so that he might decide he likes you. Be in his presence to gain familiarity. Wait until your cause needs his authority, and when he summons, you will be comfortable in his presence.

Should the king speak to you during your warm-up time, it will be to ask a question. Put all thoughts of your cause away, unless that is what is asked for. Answer with as few words as possible. Remain humble, courteous, and tactful. Refrain from asking questions in return but hang on every word the king speaks. You are here to get comfortable, not promote yourself.

If you have not had the time and opportunity to do your homework, remember that the king is human like the rest of us. There is no substitute for preparation, but your sense of unease can be diminished if you develop the habit of treating all people equally. Everyone has the same three built-in motivators: pleasure, possessions, and pride. Using these with the king is too unpredictable for launching a cause. To gain the needed authority, you want to activate this person's purpose motivator. This person just happens to be the king. The king may be a servant to the people, a tyrant, or a useless playboy, but he is first human. A wise person will treat subordinates as kings and queens, and a king as a subordinate.

Though time is of the essence, you may be in a cultural environment where formal greeting protocols are expected. Obey the cultural norms for this encounter. Typically, the normative approach to a king is to give an overt indication of your submission to his authority. Knowing your place will make this act of subservience easy to accomplish. Though bowing and kneeling have fallen out of use in most settings, there will be other ritualized forms to this greeting.

I have one member of my current team who has the habit of greeting me with a simple, "Hey, boss." Not because I told him to; he does it as a natural part of his leadership. In the past, he has held positions of authority several levels above my current position. As a leader himself, he understands the importance of ritual greetings. He recognizes the need to encourage my team, which is also his team, to be aware of the authority structure. His greeting strengthens his ability to lead within the team, by strengthening the authority structure that supplies the authority for his leadership. He has done this since day one, and although he has not yet received a promotion, in my absence, the team turns to him for guidance.

Listen to me answer the phone when I know who the caller is, and you will not know if the caller is a subordinate or the king. They all get the same simple greeting, "Yes, sir." Or "Yes, ma'am," delivered with a smile and a hint of anticipation of meeting a need. My team glows when they hear it, and the king is also honored by it. This is one method I use to be ready to enter the king's presence, because I treat them all equally.

When being brought before the king, greet him correctly. Observe any rituals, or your well-prepared cause will die here. The Bible's accounting of the story of David and Goliath does not contain the details of this greeting, but I strongly suggest that you not overlook the humble approach to the throne. Find some way to indicate your submission in your greeting.

In the king's presence is not a new place for David. At the time he fought with Goliath, David had only recently returned from being Saul's armor bearer and harp player (see 1 Samuel 16 for details on David's employment with Saul). "And David was the youngest: and the three eldest followed Saul. But David went and returned from Saul to feed his father's sheep at Bethlehem" (1 Samuel 17:14, 15). David did not know everything about Saul from the limited exposure he had, but he knew enough to be comfortable championing his cause quickly, concisely, and completely.

QUICKLY

Do an internet search for "thirty-second me" and/or "elevator pitch." You will discover a multitude of instructional sites designed to help you reduce your entire life into a thirty-second presentation. These sites are a good place to start if you need to figure out how to get all your ideas into a small presentation, but they are not enough. Thirty seconds is too long. You need one sentence, ready to use when the moment arrives. Do not wait until the king asks. Decide what you will say in advance. Keep your cause in a sentence.

Hopefully, at this point in your leadership path, you have written down your purpose and committed fully to it. Stop reading and get that done now if you are still unsure. Purpose, plus problem, plus proposed solution equals a cause. The king knows about the problem and has several solutions in mind already. Only a leader's purpose can change the decision equation. Without it, you will be just one more voice of uninspired council.

After the greeting, be ready to act. Kings are typically very busy people, and they do not waste time. You may be asked a question about your cause, or the greeting may simply be complete. Either way, jump in now and deliver the sentence you have been preparing. David has not had a lot of time to prepare but champions his cause well with a simple sentence composed of two ideas—a problem and a solution.

And when the words were heard which David spake, they rehearsed them before Saul: and he sent for him. And David said to Saul, Let no man's heart fail because of him; thy servant will go and fight with this Philistine. (1 Samuel 17:31–32)

Saul calls. David comes and gets straight to the point. The king will not always give an indication to you when he is ready to hear about your cause, but he did summon you for that purpose. Be bold, and out of respect for the king's time, get to the point quickly.

CONCISELY

The content of that sentence is usually the sticking point for most leaders. We tend to want to explain our reasoning. This is our pride of person seeking validation from the king. But our objective is delegation, not validation. Set pride aside and consider only the authority you need to act. Then choose your words with care, like David.

Circumspectly choose the right words and put them in the right order. If you want to lead, you must become articulate. Communicating your cause effectively requires understanding the impact of your words. Consider these phrases:

- Do not be afraid of him.
- We should not fear him.

- He is no one to fear.
- "Let no man's heart fail because of him" (1 Samuel 17:32).

"Do not be afraid" accuses the king of cowardice and reminds him of his failure to act. "We should not fear him" places the king and David on the same level and then tells the king to follow David's lead. "He is no one to fear" focuses on someone who is not in the room, and the statement is a lie because Goliath is frightening. But "Let no man's heart fail because of him" (1 Samuel 17:32) points indirectly to the problem that has immobilized the army, does not use the word *fear*, gives credit for the failure to everyone, and places the blame on Goliath.

Yes, you need to be very circumspect when creating the perfect sentence. Better still, take the time to learn effective communication. Then, at a moment's notice, you are less likely to misspeak. Learned skills like this improve performance but are still not a substitute for preparation. This will take practice and study. Your purpose will need to be significant to convince you to take the extra time to learn good communication skills. With time, accurate communication will become second nature. Get to work now on improving, so you will be ready when you meet the king.

When crafting your cause sentence for the king, you can follow David's simple pattern. First, clearly identify the problem that is to be solved, without blaming the king for creating the problem. Then humble yourself and admit you need the king's authority. David labels himself Saul's servant not as a reminder to Saul but as an admission that David cannot act without Saul's delegation. Then offer your personalized solution. The king does not need your full battle plan. He wants to know what action you are going to take after receiving his authority.

David offers to go and fight. Simple action verbs that convey clear intent. Note that there is no mention of defeating Goliath, then taking the army across the valley to destroy the Philistines. Only to go and fight. David has reduced his cause to the first actions of the cause. Had he asked Saul to promote him to the rank of general so that he might lead the army to victory in Saul's absence, he would have been refused. Remember that David's cause is to remove the reproach from Israel, not get promoted, get wealthy, marry the king's daughter, gain freedom for his father's house, and live happily ever after. While crafting your cause sentence, keep your eye on the target, remove self-promotion from your thinking, and reduce the authority you are asking for to only that which is necessary to get started. Offer to go and fight.

COMPLETELY

Deliver your sentence and stop talking. When defending your cause, be wise like David and allow the king opportunity to work through the normal dynamics of dealing with a new idea: rejection, questioning, reasoning, buy-in. Until this moment, everyone in the Israeli army has refused to go and fight with Goliath, including the king. Step one in the process of dealing with a new idea is rejection, and Saul needs time to conclude that David's solution will not work. When you present your cause to the king, he will reject it, at first. Be ready for it and wait patiently for it.

Giving the king time to process your one sentence and reject your idea requires your silence. Do not launch into the story of how you came to champion this cause. Be still. Some kings are not comfortable with long silences. He may make statements that indicate he is considering the effects of the actions you suggest. If you are asked a simple one- or two-word question, answer it with the same brevity. *When? Today. How much? Four point five.* If the question is a complex sentence, it is rhetorical so do not answer. You are waiting for the statement of rejection. David gets a clear rejection from Saul.

And Saul said to David, Thou art not able to go against this Philistine to fight with him: for thou art but a youth, and he a man of war from his youth. (1 Samuel 17:33)

Agree with the king. The idea is being rejected, not the person who delivered it. Rejection is step one in the process, but it indicates that the idea is being considered. Arguing with the king will not gain his authority, nor will it repair your wounded pride. Choose to deal with the pieces of the sentence that are easy to agree with. David is young and lacks the size and the experience of war that Goliath has. These are true statements that David can easily accept. You must do the same if you are going to help the king through the next phase of dealing with this new idea, which is questioning.

Saul begins his questioning by including in his rejection statement the reasons why he is saying, "no." In sales, these are known as objections, and salespeople work to overcome objections to win the sale. If the king presents you with objections in his rejection statement, he has already moved past the rejection, and you can too.

(If you get a flat no, without these reasons, resist the urge to ask, "Why?" If you remain still, the king will explain; and if not, the king is stuck on rejecting your cause, and no amount of pleading will change his mind. This is rare but can happen. Humbly accept the rejection, return to your place and your work, and reevaluate your cause. If your purpose is larger than the problem and your statement was crafted well, then stick with it. Keep promoting your cause, until the king summons you again.)

While the conditions that Saul lists for rejecting the idea are valid, they may not be reasons to reject. Often, the areas that the king points to can even be seen as advantages. David is young, and with his smaller size, he will be able to move much faster than Goliath. While the king could easily accept this turning of disadvantage to advantage, what he really wants is proof. A precept can be derived from this: be ready to prove your cause. That proof can come from the future, the present, or the past.

Future

Pull out your crystal ball and spin a tale for the king. In some environments, the proof may come in the form of charts and graphs that display a prediction of future events based on sound reasoning. You may need to tell a story of world events and how they will unfold as other kings follow through on threats, alliances, and promised projects. Paint a picture of the king's newly improved organization after the success of the cause, to get his approval. Use any prognostication and propaganda you want for this type of proof; it is all just fantasy anyway. Make it bright, colorful, and exciting if you want the king's delegation.

All future proof is unreal because future events cannot be predicted. We do need to be able to see cause and effect chains that should produce the desired future result, which is a part of circumspect leadership. But these logic chains are not proof. When you see your cause fully realized, what are the chances that the prediction will hold true, and what are the possible consequences when they do not come true?

We know David defeats Goliath and removes the reproach, but he might have chosen not to if he had foreseen all the consequences. An accurate prediction for the king would include Saul's response to David's success. David became a threat to Saul, and the king would eventually put a bounty on David's head. If the king accepts your fairy tale, he may yet give you a delegation, but the results you promised may not be achievable, because they are not predictable.

Some kings may insist on future proof. These kings are typically those who have kept their authority tight, always pushing responsibility and accountability out to their subordinates. For these kings, failure is an acceptable risk if there is a scapegoat. What the king wants as proof is that no adverse consequences of the cause can be laid at his feet. Give him that proof, and you will have your delegation, but since not all the consequences of success are predictable, you will likely become the king's enemy if you succeed or fail. I counsel against using the future for proof because it is fantasy.

Present

Using the present as proof for the king involves identifying the conditions that exist that ensure success. These conditions could be market-driven indexes that have reached an all-time high or low. Often having the right people, trained in the right skills, together in the same location is the proof that is needed. For some kings, you might simply point them to a star that has reached the right point in the sky, an owl that flew overhead, or a dream you had last night. Prove to the king's satisfaction that the time is right, and you will get your delegation.

Success in getting the delegation this way requires understanding the king's superstitions. Get him to put on his rose-colored glasses, and your cause will gain his support. The proof may demonstrate an overwhelming advantage for the cause, because of preparation and maturation of events, but preparation mitigates risk; it does not eliminate it. The chances of success improve as risk is mitigated, but the risk of failure still exists.

Present proofs rely on the gambler's fallacy. Hand the king a coin and tell him that the last ten flips were heads, so he should bet his kingdom that the next flip will be tails. How likely is this king to look past reason and flip the coin? If your king is a risk taker who has risen in the authority structure by taking chances and winning, your delegation is assured. More conservative kings who have risen by circumspectly avoiding risk will send you away empty-handed.

Be bold and let the excitement of taking a risk get your blood pressure up. Like the fairy tales of future proofs, theatrics can often be enough to tip the scale. Even the most daring of kings will need a little emotional push. Gaining your delegation, never forget that the king's decision is based on the gambler's fallacy—a lie. Succeed or fail, you may answer to the king if he ever sees through your deception. I counsel against using present proof.

Past

Proof based on facts that will convince the king is best found in the past. David has not one but two stories to convey to the king that will help overcome the objections to his age, size, and experience. These events that he conveys to the king are examples of how he has faced similar situations in the past and prevailed. Experience is the best indicator of future success.

"And David said unto Saul, Thy servant kept his father's sheep, and there came a lion, and a bear, and took a lamb out of the flock: And I went out after him, and smote him, and delivered it out of his mouth: and when he arose against me, I caught him by his beard, and smote him, and slew him. Thy servant slew both the lion and the bear: and this uncircumcised Philistine shall be as one of them, seeing he hath defied the armies of the living God. David said moreover, The LORD that delivered me out of the paw of the lion, and out of the paw of the bear, he will deliver me out of the hand of this Philistine. And Saul said unto David, Go, and the LORD be with thee." (1 Samuel 17:34–37)

Proof from the past is established in fact, not fantasy. As a shepherd, David has already had to face some impossible enemies. The word *smote*, struck with a firm blow from a weapon or the hand, is the same word used to describe the stone striking Goliath. The skills and courage needed for these two encounters demonstrate a likelihood of success against Goliath.

David is giving Saul a play-by-play of previous events that demonstrate his attack plan. Being young, he was fast enough to catch up with a lion and a bear. As a man of war, he had learned to use a sling well enough to smite the lion and the bear while running after them. And as a man of war, when the lion turned and came after him, he did not faint but grabbed it by the beard and killed it. David has no embellishments or exaggerations, just the facts. Then he ties those facts to the present need to show how he will defeat Goliath.

We see also in David's answer an unwavering commitment to his purpose. Though triumph over a lion and a bear would typically be the cause of a tremendous amount of pride, David is careful to give credit to God. No pride of person, possessions, or place is evident in his recounting. Purpose is what backs the recounting, without the need for embellishment or exaggeration to inflate pride.

David wants to remove the reproach from Israel, and he has a simple plan. Stay away from Goliath, hit him with rocks until he falls, and then move in for the kill. His recounting of the fights with the lion and the bear are not bragging but a battle plan. An approach to the problem that Saul has not considered, involves no risk to the king, and has been proven effective.

Because proof from the past is based on fact instead of fallacy, I counsel using this type of proof to win your delegation. Future and present proofs can be effective with the right king, but the results are unpredictable. Some kings may even insist that you demonstrate future proof that shows success. But the best constructed statistical model cannot predict the future, nor prove success by current conditions. Only the past provides fact-based reasoning to demonstrate expected success. Use the past as your proof if possible.

Getting your king's blessing will require proof. Do your homework and prepare proof from your past. Let your purpose guide the selection and the recounting of the proof. Do not embellish, exaggerate, or posture. Tell the story, tie it to the current problem, and wait for the king to decide again. If your proof is accepted, the king will move into the reasoning stage of dealing with new ideas.

THE KING'S HELP

You will know that the shift has happened when the king begins "improving" your battle plan. Though this is your cause, backed by your purpose, the king will attempt to satisfy his own motivational ideas by changing the plan. This is good news for you as the leader, because the king has now accepted the cause as worth fighting for.

This would be another inconvenient time to argue with the king. He has been courteous enough to consider your new idea, so pay him the same courtesy. In the case of a king who is also a quality leader his ideas may be useful. Most of the time, the ideas will be inspired by one of the built-in motivators, which will make them inconsistent with your purpose. Listen attentively anyway. Let the king get his thoughts all out on the table, and it should be easy enough to demonstrate how these may not be consistent with your cause.

And Saul armed David with his armour, and he put an helmet of brass upon his head; also he armed him with a coat of mail. And David girded his sword upon his armour, and he assayed to go; for he had not proved it. And David said unto Saul, I cannot go with these; for I have not proved them. And David put them off him. (1 Samuel 17:38, 39)

David does not try to stop Saul from offering his armor. At that time in Israel, there were only two swords, Saul's, and his son Jonathan's. Armor would be as rare a commodity and wearing it in combat would be a distinct advantage. We are not told why Saul offers his armor, and I do not think it matters. This was the king's effort to participate by contributing his reasonable ideas.

The armor was not part of David's plan for the cause. David tried it on to ensure that he gave the king's idea a chance to work. When they both saw it would not work, David had the delegation he needed and his original plan. The king has worked through the reasoning stage and has settled into the last phase of buy-in. David has the full authority of the king to step out on the battlefield to fight the giant with a slingshot.

Delegation Achieved

You may find it easy to sway the king to support your cause. Carefully approach your king, prepared for the encounter. Present your cause quickly, concisely, and completely. Give the king his proof and ease him from rejections, through questioning and reasoning, to buy-in. When you have the authority you need, do as David did and get to work.

Precepts

- Causes need the king's authority.
- Keep your cause in a sentence.
- Prove your cause.

5

FIVE STONES

Pursuing a cause brings you to this unsettling moment. Your purpose created a cause and won you the authority to act. Attached to the authority are responsibility and accountability. For the first time, you are on your own, with nothing standing between you and the accomplishment of your cause—except a giant. Until now, all your efforts have been theoretical, but action is now required to make the cause real.

And he took his staff in his hand, and chose him five smooth stones out of the brook, and put them in a shepherd's bag which he had, even in a scrip; and his sling was in his hand: and he drew near to the Philistine. (1 Samuel 17:40)

Once a delegation is received, planning time is over. If you are fully committed to your cause, all that is needed now is action. David took, chose, put, and drew. Simple actions that describe a series of preparation steps that led to battle. No time for delay because delegations require actions.

Your team cannot follow if you are not out in front, and they will not act until you do. In the initial stages of accomplishing your cause, you should base your actions on the work you have been doing. Familiar actions tend to bring us back to patterns of behavior that have sustained us, but something about the world you were living in needed to change. The change will require patterns in your behavior to change first. Because thought precedes action, breaking old patterns of behavior requires new patterns of thought.

Leaders often fail because they assume that the plan that won them a delegation is the plan they need to execute. Though war may not have been an outcome you were working toward, you are now ready to engage in your first battle. Take stock before moving forward. Is your purpose foremost in your thoughts? Does your cause align with that purpose? Do you have the authority to act? Do you have your weapons ready? Is your plan sound, and will it lead to victory? While this last question should have a solidly affirmative answer if the others are affirmative, that plan is already no longer relevant.

In chapter 1, you began by evaluating the world situation around you at the time that you chose to lead. At that moment, you had no cause, no authority, and no plan. The situation has changed, and so the plan of action you developed is no longer relevant. This concept is extensively discussed in military tactics. The basic concept is that no battle plan survives first contact with the enemy. No plan survives its birth because implementation of the plan changes the situation.

The moment you enter the battlefield, you must abandon your original plan and choose moment to moment the actions required to accomplish the cause in support of your purpose. You must think quickly, accurately, and decisively. For David, his first action on entering the battlefield forced Goliath to change his plan. Goliath's original plan was to maintain balance and stasis, not actually confront anyone in open combat, and the entrance of someone in front of him destroyed his original plan. David's plan was to treat Goliath like the bear and lion, but Goliath does not immediately attack and then run away as they did. Neither Goliath nor David can execute the plan that they started with because the situation changed when David stepped out.

When you stepped out on the battlefield, you became the cog in the machine that refused to keep turning in a predictable way. The world as experienced by everyone around you changed at that moment. From this point forward, each of your actions must be in response to the newly changed conditions. A new way of thinking that is predicated on swift decisions followed by immediate actions is now required. Success in changing the world will depend on you outthinking your opponents.

Simple patterns of repetitive thought decrease decision time. My favorite pattern to follow for fast decisions is OODA: observe, orient, decide, act. Militaries teach this pattern to help reduce decision times in combat. Colonel John Boyd, USAF, is given credit for originating this pattern, which increased pilot reaction times, giving them an advantage in combat even against superior enemies.

You may be thinking that this is too simple an idea to have much impact, and besides, you are not in combat. The way that you think about the world around you follows patterns that you have learned since birth. Change is only possible if you learn a new way of thinking. That ideal self-image you have been working toward, and coming up short of, will only be achieved with improvement. Since the pattern of your thinking has created the person you are, it cannot help you change to become that ideal. A new pattern will be required to create a purposeful change.

The person that you are was programmed by your thinking through repetitive acts followed by consequences. You cannot escape the cause-and-effect world that we are designed to live in. If repetition created this person, it cannot also produce the ideal. Follow the same pattern of thinking, and you get the same result. Let go of your resistance to change and try using the simple OODA pattern to get moving in the direction you want to go.

Observation and experience taught me that patterned thought is necessary to change patterned behavior. Patterned behavior in combat would be disastrous. In everyday life, it creates the world around us. My patterns interact with the patterns of those I encounter like so many cogs in a machine. My decisions have consequences that affect everyone on the planet. So, when I want to change something in the world, I start by changing my thinking.

Learning about the OODA loop more than a decade ago brought me to the point of finally authoring this book. I had no need for a large course of study to implement OODA, though there is plenty of material available to increase effectiveness. I was introduced to it in a fifteen-minute presentation that had nothing to do with flying planes, and I lean on it daily when stress and competing interests threaten to move me off my purpose. My decisions are still my own, but they can happen much faster if I utilize OODA. For maximum impact, I teach it to my teams and actively promote its use.

In fact, without deciding in advance to do so, I have authored the book to this point based on the OODA pattern of thinking. In the leadership journey, we first *observed* the world as it is, in chapter 1 before we chose to lead. Orientation came next with know your place, know your people, know your purpose, and even the ideas of motivation. The discussion on motivating with a cause is where a *decision* is made. And then *act* has taken us from the decision to the invitation to speak with the king.

Not only is the big picture patterned on OODA, but there are many micro OODA opportunities within that bigger pattern. When Eliab attacked David as he was building support for his cause, David could have used an OODA loop to make the correct decision. *Observe: was that a physical attack? Orient: why is he attacking, who is watching, what will my father think, will this conversation remove any reproach, and how can I remove the threat? Decide: I should defend my cause, not myself. Act:* is there not a cause (1 Samuel 17:29)? We are not told what David's thoughts were, but my OODA loop would have looked something like this if faced with the same situation.

You will be surprised how often your thoughts return to this pattern in stressful situations. Writing is not currently my full-time job. Work occasionally requires me to visit my customers at their homes. Having been invited to visit one property while the owner was away for the day, I asked about the dog and was assured he was safely inside the house. My instructions were to come through the big gate and walk through to the back. Halfway to the backyard, the *other* dog came my way from the shadows of a doorway.

Immediately the panic stopped with the observation that I was still standing. Orientation continued: forty feet back to the gate; dog approximately eighty pounds, older and moving slower, still fast enough to outrun me; in my hand is a cell phone (no help); no people around to watch me get eaten; the dog is now three feet away. I decided to remember everything I had learned throughout life about such encounters and calmly meet the threat. Action meant standing straight with arms extended out from my sides, showing no fear and feeling only a little. I paused and let him bark without reacting. Without making eye contact or turning around, I slowly backed away toward the gate, and he stood his ground. Only when the gate was closed again did he charge the fence to make sure I stayed out. I calmly walked around the side of the property, where the *other* gate led to the backyard and continued with my work.

We are not told that David used an OODA loop, but we can take a closer look at what an OODA loop may have looked like. Let's take a closer look at observation, orientation, decision, and action to see how they might help you. I will show how each step may have helped David out as well.

OBSERVE

Organizing your thoughts will disrupt the pattern of stimulus and response that has produced the person that you are. OODA works well for this disruption because it decreases the amount of time to decide when under stress. For fighter pilots, that could be anything from a threat warning alarm to a missile exploding nearby. At that moment immediately following the stimulus, the pilot's observation begins the OODA process. Since they are flying a plane, a simple question like "Is the plane still flying?" starts the process. The answer to the question is binary (yes or no) and sums up the most important aspects of the moment.

Observations are objective and do not require any emotions. Stimuli such as receiving a delegation of authority to pursue a cause, produce moments of vulnerability. Vulnerability because patterns of thought from the past produce an emotional reaction that adds nothing to observations. Pilots who respond emotionally to an enemy firing at their plane will not likely make it back to base. Leaders who habitually react emotionally to delegations or other stimuli fail before they begin.

Happiness is a good thing, and celebrating successes helps create new patterns of successful behavior, but celebration produces no progress toward success in the cause. Pride, swelling up to produce a sense of elation at receiving the delegation, is a distraction a leader cannot afford. Celebratory moments come later; for now, this delegation requires action. A simple binary question frames the beginning of an OODA process that provides a response that moves the cause forward. "Do I have the authority I need?"

Fear is another common emotional reaction in these moments. Leaders who have experienced the pain and suffering that is part of leadership may find the motivator of pain avoidance taking control. Because fear is such a powerful motivator, just knowing that unpleasantness is coming will not be enough to stop the avoidance behavior. A question, inserted before fear takes root, can short-circuit the avoidance pattern, and allow a response that will move the leader toward the coming unpleasantness instead of away from it. "Is the giant still there?"

If you are following a good leader, they may help you through a fearful moment. I remember one unsought delegation that came my way in my early twenties. Recently out of the navy, I won a supervisory position with a small team to lead. After a year of stretching my wings and learning how to seek out delegations, I succeeded in creating several improvements in the team. Then someone in upper management was arrested for embezzlement (possession and pride motivators have some dark outcomes). I was selected as a candidate to fill the vacated position. Before delegating management authority to me, the company president asked me what more I would change. With the exaggerated excitement of youth, I said we would double our current revenue generation (this is why your cause statement needs to be short, to the point, and well planned). He asked for proof of that assertion, and I had none. Suddenly I was gripped with fear, expecting the pain that would follow, because I had no idea how much additional revenue I could generate. The president of the company saw the crippling response and reassured me that simply maintaining the current level of productivity would be acceptable. While he did delegate to me the authority I needed to hold the status quo, he delegated the authority to create change to a mentor he assigned to me from his executive team. When you delegate to your team members, watch for changes in posture, skin tone, eye contact, and voice inflection that may indicate fear and change their motivation quickly. A wise leader will also find simple questions that can replace fear in their own response patterns. "Do I know that for sure?"

When you get your delegation, the excitement of what comes next might overwhelm you. Fight-or-flight responses that keep you safe when out hunting and gathering produce powerful emotions. A pilot who reacts with fight or flight either ignores risk and attacks or pulls the ejection handle when the plane is still flyable. Leaders who allow the fight reaction to the delegation might take brash action and assume massive risk with their first decision, leaving their cause smoldering in the ensuing crash. I have seen the flight response cause would-be leaders to disappear entirely, abandoning their delegation rather than acting. If the reaction is not immediately disastrous, the cortisol released in the body will generate unhealthy levels of stress that cloud judgment. Slow down and ask an observation question to insert an OODA loop and generate a proper response. "Is my team ready?"

The most common reaction to an unexpected stimulus like a missile chasing your plane or receipt of a delegation is denial. Instead of accepting reality, we reject it and seek out alternative explanations. Thoughts like *That did not just happen, Why did that happen?* or *Did that just happen to me?* lead into the realm of the irrational. Fire investigators recognize that there are always some people who, if in a public building that is on fire, move toward the fire instead of an exit. We cannot know what motivates them for certain because they do not survive, but they might think a simple thought like, *That cannot really be a fire.* That thought causes them to investigate instead of fleeing. That is how destructive this descent into the irrational can be. A purpose that is not large enough to hold the entirety of the delegation can easily push a leader into denial. Denial will produce decisions based on paranoia, suspicion, and irrational curiosity. Refuse to explore the irrational and ask a simple question to get an OODA loop started. "Am I still breathing?"

We are not told what question David asked himself after receiving Saul's delegation. His reaction could have been to celebrate or run and hide. Samuel's account of the events provides us only with the simple actions that David took. Samuel writes them in a single sentence, and the only embellishment is of the scrip, which serves to emphasize the ordinary, familiar nature of what he watched David do. The observer saw simple, everyday preparatory actions. Those actions are calm, rational, preparatory, and familiar, which is our only indication that David's thoughts are on his purpose and his cause to remove the reproach.

Do not react. Respond. Reacting produces emotion-driven decisions that are not likely in alignment with purpose but aligned with pleasure, pride, or avoidance of pain. Allowing emotions to drive decisions will destroy a cause before it begins. Responding to the reality of the moment, the weight of the delegation, and the needs of the cause will produce the right decisions. Make your observation by asking a simple yes or no question.

ORIENT

A simple observation like *the plane is still flying* will not be enough information to make an effective decision before acting. A pilot's decisions always include altitude, speed, direction, vertical orientation, fuel level, and a myriad of other tiny details that they review every few seconds. More to the point in combat are the details of what the enemy has done, is doing, and is likely to do. Orienting on the target of action follows observation.

Samuel does not know what David is thinking, so again he gives us a simple statement that describes the action, "he drew near to the Philistine" (1 Samuel 17:40). Observations are all about controlling thought patterns; orientation is about deciding. Observations can be made at a distance, but orienting will require you to get up close and personal. This is a narrowing of focus that broadens thoughts into an increasing set of parameters until a decision happens. There will be no need to press for a decision because increasing awareness narrows actions until only one or more than two remains.

One or more than two might seem an odd statement. Though a binary question having a yes/no answer triggers a good observation, orientation needs more options. A binary decision with two actions implies a fifty-fifty situation where either of the two leads to good action. This scenario does happen, but I avoid it at all costs, often asking a new observational question and scrapping the OODA loop I am in. When a coin flip is all that is required to make a workable decision, the other side of the gambler's fallacy will take hold. The other side is assuming that, because the last ten flips of the coin were heads, then the next flip is also likely to be heads because there is a pattern of only heads. A pattern of success cannot continue forever on binary decisions. I have learned that if I reach a binary option, one of my premises developed in orientation is wrong. A yes or no answer is best to start an OODA loop, but I council against accepting a binary decision option.

These binary options often crop up when being challenged with an ultimatum from an opponent. The opponent chooses for you two options for actions that should both lead to a good outcome for them. Goliath has been presenting Israel with an ultimatum for the last forty days. Ultimatums are usually based on a fear motivator but often disguise one of the options with a pleasure motivator. Take this option and be crushed or take this option for a reward beyond your wildest dreams. Your opponent does not have your best interests in mind when they make the offer. Both options lead to your defeat. I recommend you reject both.

Orientation is designed to carry your thoughts rationally forward, cataloging and analyzing the world around you without emotion. Objectivity is central to a good decision-making process. Observation disrupts emotional reactions, and the response of orientation should continue to keep those emotional reactions quelled. Orientation helps the leader frame their cause into the context of the real, observable world and bring them to the point of decision.

Sarge comes to mind when I picture David's approach to Goliath. Before a church service one Sunday, Sarge and I were in the hallway ushering people into the service when the wrestling coach from a local college walked by. The man was easily six foot six, with thighs as big around as my head. A mountain of a man whose muscles rippled his clothes, Sarge may have only been five feet tall, but he was a highly trained and skilled marine as well as a committed wrestler from his youth. Sarge knew who this man was and knew he was not a threat to the gathering, but he assessed the coach with a noticeable head movement, up and down. The head movement caught my attention because, at that moment, I could tell that his focus had moved from the entire hallway full of people to this one giant among the throng, and he was intently focused. Though I was fortunate enough to have never been in combat with Sarge, I could tell this was the way he would assess a threat on the battlefield. The orientation on this single person in the crowd took less than half a second, but a large amount of information was being evaluated. Then he snapped out of it, and with a grin, he leaned over and confidently said, "I can take him." I was highly amused at this spontaneous assertion but glad he did not follow through to prove it.

As David drew near, he would have noticed the army of Israel at his back as he walked past the front lines. The army of the Philistines is in front of him, on the other side of the valley. Goliath is roaming around in the valley in front of the Israeli army, shouting his taunts. A man with a shield tall enough to protect Goliath from any projectiles is struggling to keep up with Goliath's movements. The shield would have been more than eight feet tall to cover Goliath, and that is not something that can be moved easily. Too light a shield would be like carrying a sail around, and not even wheels would help in rocky terrain. The man with the shield was a liability, not an asset.

Focusing on the target, David would have seen Goliath as Samuel presented him earlier in the story. He is armored head, body, and legs with large pieces of brass and steel. The massive spear he carried would kill without a point on it, but even with Goliath's obvious strength, it could not be thrown far. He was strong but weighed down to a point of moving with considerable effort. His range of motion was also limited in that he remained behind the shield bearer, facing the Israeli army. He was well protected from the front only and would not be able to move quickly to defend from the side or from behind.

Seen through the eyes of fear being used by the Israeli army, Goliath looked invincible. After an unemotional orientation, David would have seen that he was weighed down, vulnerable on three sides, and too slow to ward off a quick attacker. Goliath's patterned behavior worked to keep the Israeli army at bay for forty days, but that would soon change. Because it was decision time for David.

DECIDE

The most important lesson I have learned about decision-making is to never decide until a decision must be made. Changing conditions in your environment may add opportunities for action that are not present when you enter the orientation cycle of your loop. Forcing a decision early will result in a loss of opportunity. While the newly presented course of action may not be the right decision, considering it will only strengthen your resolve on the right decision. Wait for it. Orient until the right decision is reached, and then do the right thing.

Over the last thirty years of observing leaders, I have discovered that most people make decisions based on how they feel or how the action will make them feel. Attempting to lead a team to create change based on how it will make them feel will only lead to frustration—for you and your team. The leader is the model the team will follow. Emotionally led decisions seldom align with causes. Experiencing pleasure or avoiding pain leaves no room for a purpose. Some team members will push to move forward to get the reward of celebrating success, but they will easily fall off the mark without another motivator. The rest of the team will work to avoid the pain of failure. While the leader attempts to realign half the team to match their own feeling motivators, the team stands still, eventually tearing itself apart in debate. The solution is to know your purpose. Decisions should align with purpose, which gives the simple precept—do the right thing.

Doing the right thing does not mean that you know what the outcome will be. Remember that future proofs are lies because prediction is not possible. Recognizing cause and effect chains can help with decisions but should not be the primary decision factor. Your purpose is the only motivator that can help you. Irrational decisions based on future proofs will never lead to success in a cause. The right thing is a decision consistent with purpose.

This precept is often difficult to utilize because your other motivators, like emotions, get in the way. You are human, and there are always things that you want to add to your collections. Recognizing the opportunity to realize one of those ideas by making a certain decision can overwhelm you. Thinking about the pride that will come from success may be a part of what moves you forward, but your delegation was given to you to accomplish a cause. That cause has nothing to do with your pride. Knowing your purpose keeps your decisions aligned with your cause, and eventually, all the other motivational ideas are realized. Doing the right thing means aligning all decisions with your purpose to create new patterns that lead to success.

Purpose-driven decisions are clear, obvious, and rational. Orientation eliminates all possible actions till one is the obvious best action. If a binary option presents itself, then there is no obvious best action. Choosing one or the other, with no rational explanation for why, is like flipping a coin, confidently expecting heads. Good outcomes are the result of good decisions. Good decisions require evaluating many outcomes and narrowing the field until only one is the best decision. Successful leadership is always the result of the leader deciding to do the right thing.

ACT

You chose to lead, and decisions have consequences. Choosing to lead created a need to know your purpose, which I have encouraged you to review many times. That review was to ingrain it deep enough into your thinking that you can now make decisions that are consistent with that purpose without needing to review it. The time for review is over.

From this point forward, to accomplish your cause, each decision will have immediate consequences that require another immediate decision. For David, the first decision after taking Saul's armor off was to prepare. While he could not go armored, or with a sword, his purpose taught him to never go unprepared. Even now as he was about to go to battle, he had his staff, scrip, and sling with him.

If you know your place, then you have been in that place doing the work that is there. That work has led you to develop a set of skills and build a collection of tools that are as familiar to you as your fingers. These skills and tools form the base for the actions that you take in your work. *Familiar*, *comfortable*, and *expertise* are words that you might use to describe them. Do not throw them away, thinking that work on your cause will require a new set of tools. You may need some additional tools along the way, but you should start with what you already know and the tools you use every day. Another precept of leadership is to use what you know.

David has a literal giant to kill now that he has authority from Saul. He makes a wise decision to prepare not for battle but for work. His staff, shepherd's bag, and his sling are with him because they are always with him. Leaving home prepared to work was his first good action. Though he would not be tending sheep along the way to the battlefield, these three tools were his everyday implements, and they are the starting point for his actions.

I remember another unexpected delegation I received to be a part of a project team monitoring the construction of a new footbridge. The delegation came my way because I was the newest person on staff, not because of a cause I was promoting. As with any delegation I receive, I took it on with a passion, immediately requisitioning and purchasing expensive project-management software. After installing it, I quickly discovered that the installation was all that my information technology degree prepared me to do. Learning what I needed to know about project management so I could use the software took another eleven years (do not give up on learning something new). All I was required to do on this project team was to attend meetings about the progress of the project and disseminate what I discovered to my other teams, and I did not need software for that.

David used what he knew. I started by launching into a multiyear learning process that has left me better prepared to lead, but by the time I learned it, the delegation I had been given was long gone. David achieved victory before the sun went down, and the bridge was built without my help. Your cause will only be accomplished through the actions of leadership. Delegations require action. Your delegation requires immediate action, so use what you know.

Take familiar action and do it right now. If you are an expert in accounting, take a few minutes to write out a budget. List out a sequential order of steps needed to accomplish your cause if you are a coordinator. Identify a KPI and begin monitoring it for variance if you are a quality assurance expert. Use what you know to build a circuit, author a poem, calculate wind shear, bake a cake, inventory your tools, or build a new file structure on your computer. Wise first actions are familiar and fast.

For David, that would mean taking the necessary preparation steps to be ready to go to work and battle. His first action is to take his staff in his hand, which is an especially useful tool. Often it is used simply to extend the arm, allowing the shepherd to move the sheep in the direction he wants them to go. Its hooked end is useful for recovering sheep that have fallen into a hole or down a cliff. A good, sturdy staff could also be used for fording streams or vaulting between rocks in difficult terrain. It may not have been a sword, but it was a tool that David knew how to use.

Next, he chooses five smooth stones from the brook. Study the story of David and Goliath long enough, and you will discover a vast number of debates about these stones. These stones have become the source of quite a bit of mythology, but in the end, they are just projectiles for his sling. Why five? Maybe because they fit nicely in his bag. And smooth because that would work best in the sling. David used what he knew, which is the simple message of wisdom in his choosing five stones.

The scrip, or shepherd's bag, was a pouch made by sewing pieces of material together along three sides, with a long strap that could be easily hung on the shoulder. The scrip freed up a shepherd's hands to use the staff or sling. Nothing fancy, just a large serviceable bag, probably large enough to hold a lamb or two. This would be a tool that was on his shoulder at all times as a shepherd, a comfortable part of his normal apparel.

And his sling was in his hand. He was heading into battle and taking the time to get the sling ready would save a second or two on the battlefield. We do not get detailed descriptions of David's training and practice with the sling. We did see the word *smote* being used in David's recounting of the bear and lion battles. If you have read ahead in our story, you know that David will soon promise Goliath that his head is coming off today, but he has no sword with him to accomplish that promise. Only Saul and Johnathan had swords; the rest of the army was accustomed to fighting with whatever implements they had in hand. For David, that was a staff and sling. A sword will soon be needed, but David acts first with what he has.

David's delegation gave him authority to risk his life and step onto the battlefield first. Removing the reproach would require the whole army, but if they were to follow him, David would need to be out front. Many would-be leaders think that good leadership is sitting behind the lines, commanding the troops by issuing orders. David spent his time working with sheep and knew the easiest way to move them was to walk out in front. Still taking familiar action, David drew near to the enemy.

The resistance you will face should be in front of you, blocking progress at this point. No resistance would mean a cause that will not change anything. So, resistance is a good thing because it indicates you have something to fight for. Now is the one time in your leadership where you need to take a risk. A calculated risk, but there will be some degree of danger to you if your purpose is broad enough. Overcoming that resistance will be the starting point of building your team, but first, they need to know what this confrontation is all about.

David has Goliath where he wants him but does not charge. Instead, he draws near and waits for Goliath to go through his regular routine. David needs Goliath to demonstrate his reproach so that the members of both armies know why this is happening.

TIME TO ACT AGAIN

Goliath has kept the Israeli army at bay by presenting a binary option that has nothing but bad outcomes. He convinced each member of the Israeli army that they could either cower in fear or come and face him in single combat. David does the right thing by refusing to accept the binary situation. Samuel tells us that he drew near, which was not one of Goliath's options. If motivated by the promised rewards or pride, he might have charged out from behind a bush into a headlong attack. David's purpose is centered on doing God's will, not choosing between Goliath's options. So, David did the right thing, presented himself as an enemy, and waited to be challenged.

To remove the reproach, David needs the whole army. Earlier, he spread the message of his cause to those in his immediate part of the army, which led to his invitation to speak with the king. Now he wants the cause to be announced to both armies. David's expressed cause is not to demonstrate how God can use the small to destroy the large, though He can. The cause aims to remove reproach. For this message to get through, David needs Goliath to make the first move and either repent or attack. David is simply acting to fulfill the cause by taking actions consistent with his purpose.

PRECEPTS

- Delegations require actions.
- Do the right thing.
- Use what you know.

6

---•---

GIVE A VISION

Your team needs to know the plan. If you have been defending your cause, then you have also been dealing with the rejection coming from those who hear it. Anticipation of that rejection blunts desire and generates timidity. Cast that aside. Bold defense of your cause backed by proof for the king won the authority to act. Some of your team members have already worked through their rejection and started questioning the validity of the cause. Give them a reasonable plan to execute, and they will follow.

Though you have the king's authority, you still need the team's buy-in. Those who follow permit you to make decisions on their behalf. They submit to your authority in at least a small portion of their lives. This submission is a delegation of authority to you from those who follow. Authority that you will then delegate to other team members. This mechanism of tradeoffs in authority pulls teams together as the members submit their authority to the team pool, then receive a delegation containing more authority than was submitted. Though the delegation comes from you, it contains authority delegated from other members of the team, which has team members submitted to one another. This mechanism is not a natural process, and it requires a leader to make it happen.

Submitting to authority is simple but not easy. We want to retain self-willed control of our own lives. Knowing authority places us in an awkward position as an independent, self-willed person. Knowledge should dictate action, but when confronted with the need to defer to the person with authority, we look for reasons to retain what authority we have. We expect that submission means giving away some control in our lives to another person and gaining nothing in return; however, if we submit, we open ourselves up to receive a delegation, and the delegation gives authority we did not originally have. Through that delegation, we enlist others who submit, giving us more authority that we did not have originally. Step one in gaining authority is to submit to it.

This simple mechanism of submission is the reason that people will not come together in the absence of a leader. If two self-willed, independent actors meet, neither submits to the other. Introductions may establish an authority hierarchy, but that is no guarantee that either submits. The two cannot work together unless one establishes leadership. No leader, no collaboration, no change.

Put a handful of strangers in a room at lunchtime. On one side of the room is a table with a collection of grocery sacks on it. Provide no instructions and establish no authority structure for this group of strangers. How long will it take them to organize to prepare lunch from the groceries on the table? They will most likely leave the room hungry and angry for having had their time wasted. Yet, if one of the strangers decides to lead, suggests that they might eat while waiting for what comes next, some of the group is likely to submit to that leadership, and everyone will eat. The most likely outcome though is no lunch.

One team I attempted to pull together failed because of this fear of submission. There were four of us, who had the intelligence, drive, and ambition to acquire a prized legal certification. None of us were attorneys. As a team, we could have transformed the face of business in our local community and advanced the cause to spread around the world. We lacked only a single source for the vision. One of us had to be the leader that the others submitted to.

Ten people were in the training class out of a group of more than one hundred who were offered the opportunity. I scheduled a meeting with the three who seemed most likely to complete the certification. We took turns presenting ideas of what a business based around the certification would look like. We discussed the possibilities, explored the needed funding, and evaluated the workflows. In the end, I pulled it all together with a complete marketing plan and estimations of the profits that could be shared between us. We had a complete business plan, and I presented a clear vision of how to move forward. We left the meeting still unsure what would happen next.

Over the next two weeks, I arranged one-on-one meetings with each of them for the expressed purpose of getting their submission to me as the leader of the group. What I discovered surprised me, because I assumed that anyone who would work as hard as we were to gain the certification would also recognize the need for a leader, but not so. The first one I met with did not understand the need for a leader and thought we could just all be leaders in our area of specialty. My next colleague was sure we could all be equals in authority, and by debate and voting, we would make group decisions and enjoy doing it. The last refused to have anyone be the leader, including himself, but if we were talking about getting paid a comfortable income (which turned out to be twice what the business plan said we could support), he was on board for that.

Most causes end this way, with the leader moving on solo to defend the cause alone. I acquired the certification, as did one of the others, but since no one was leading, we never met again as a team. Since the cause was in line with my purpose, I arranged to teach the material to others at a local community college, hoping to develop some new team members. The cause had an immediate need, but not a single student signed up for the class. After a year of attempting to pull a team together, I abandoned the cause and did not renew the certification.

This failed cause has not changed my purpose in life. Though it was a noble cause, it was only a vehicle for my purpose. An important missing piece was a delegation from the king. There was no king to approach who could provide anything we lacked. In essence, I was attempting to make myself the king, which would require submission from the others in the group. A leader cannot act without authority. We were four independent actors meeting to plan our future together, supporting a cause of great relevance but without an established authority structure. Only two of us acquired the certification, and none of us ever used the training in any direct way. This is the most common outcome for encounters of self-willed people without submission to a leader.

My purpose was still intact, so I found new causes to work on that had kings to solicit. A delegation from any king is easier to work with than starting from scratch. I discovered that making myself a king is a little more difficult. Historically, kings established their authority through privileged birth or extreme willingness to do violence. I was born to privilege in that I had two parents with well-defined purposes in life, but wealth and power were not a part of my lineage. Since I tend to avoid violence, finding a king to submit to is usually my best place to start with any cause.

David is in a valley filled with independent actors. The entire army of the Philistines represents a reproach against God, and to remove them, David will need the Israeli army to help. In the next few verses, we will see a simple, predictable, repeatable pattern that can be used to gather any team together for a cause. Watch as David gets out front, receives a challenge, and publicly announces a simple plan.

GET OUT FRONT

You will need the help of your team to fulfill your cause, and they need to be ready to fight. If your purpose created a cause that will change the world, then you will be in conflict with the leaders who have made the world what it is. Expect resistance and use it to help your team understand what needs to be done. Be cautious and move forward to find the enemy.

And the Philistine came on and drew near unto David; and the man that bare the shield went before him. And when the Philistine looked about, and saw David, he disdained him: for he was but a youth, and ruddy, and of a fair countenance. (1 Samuel 17:41, 42)

Goliath focuses his attention on David, as do both armies. Goliath has the authority to act and for the last forty days has been terrifying the army of Israel. David has the authority to take action to stop Goliath. Each has taken up a position in front of their army, demonstrating another precept that leaders get out front.

Over the last thirty years, I have been surprised by how many would-be leaders think leadership is done from behind the scenes. You want your team to *follow* your lead. The word *follow* means to go or come after a person who is in front of you. If a team is to follow, then naturally the leader will be out front. Your delegation may have come with a corner office on the sixth floor, but if your team is in the basement, then go there. If they are at the job site, you need to be there. If they are on the battlefield, then you need to go to the conflict. Whatever opposition they are going to face needs to reach you first if you expect them to follow.

Back-office leaders work on agendas, not causes. Those agendas focus on realizing inborn motivational ideas—pleasure, possessions, or pride. Back-office leaders want to enjoy their days and will spend as much time away from the office as in it. They work hard to gain the means to purchase that perfect house/car/boat/vacation. Getting the next promotion seems the only objective worth focusing on. These agendas are seldom expressed to the team, since it is none of their business and because the back-office leader knows the team is not interested in these ideas. So, the agenda becomes an urgent necessity and a secret obsession.

Though the focus of the cause escapes me, I remember one bold university student who got my attention if not my submission. As a staff member at the university, I had the occasional social duty of attending celebrations around the campus. This celebration was well attended with a diverse group of more than a hundred people, representing a cross-section of the university and local community.

The young man arrived at the front door late and immediately began explaining his tardiness to the person nearest the door as though they were longtime friends. His voice was large, and he used it well to ensure that anyone nearby would hear. Gaining my attention, as well as the attention of several others, he explained how a meeting regarding the progress of his cause kept him later than expected but that the meeting ended auspiciously. I noticed that while he was speaking to his new friend, he was pitching his voice louder to reach those who had already given their attention. As he spoke, he made friendly eye contact with each of us eavesdroppers, giving a conspiratorial wink or nod to each. He included everyone who would listen in on the conversation, and once his cause had been presented, he excused himself and moved off.

Several minutes later, I heard his voice rise from another part of the room. Though his position had changed the story he was sharing, as a way of introducing his cause was word-for-word the same. I turned to see that he had a group of three friends now and another five interested people. As I watched, each got the same wink or nod to include them as close associates in support of his cause. When the speech was complete, he moved on to another part of the room.

During the third telling, he caught me watching from the other side of the room, made eye contact, grinned broadly, and shrugged. I noticed after this retelling that he had the undivided attention of a prominent person who was not a university employee. Even with my casual observation, I saw him move this person away from the crowd as he continued his plea in a much quieter tone of voice.

Even after retelling this story, I cannot remember what the cause was, but I do remember the prominent person writing a check and handing it over. This young man's cause sounded like a good idea, and it was well presented. After the third retelling, most everyone in the room had heard about the cause, and no doubt several had repeated it to others. By the time the prominent person received special attention, the cause might have seemed the most pressing issue facing the world today because it was on everyone's lips. The truth about the young man's agenda was announced by his departing the gathering after receiving the check. He had everyone's attention and could have rallied us into a single team to right the horrible wrong, but all he wanted was money. The person giving him the check may have been interested in supporting the cause or may have simply wanted the loud-voiced interloper to leave. The young man worked his agenda, received his money, and cared not which motivated the giver.

Follow David's example. He set aside the promised rewards, choosing instead a cause backed by his purpose. David put off unfamiliar armor and weapons, taking instead the familiar tools of a working shepherd onto the battlefield. He acted according to the cause he was promoting, to remove a reproach from Israel. The reproach began with Goliath, so David simply walked out to meet him, putting himself in harm's way but also positioning himself out front.

To get out front, your cause may not require physically confronting the giant, but you still need to seek out the coming conflict. You want to change the world. The interlocking behavior patterns of the people you encounter created the circumstances of that world. Changing those circumstances changes the comfortable world they expect. Some of them work hard to create and maintain these circumstances. Your cause requires the circumstances and therefore all of those people to change. Conflict is inevitable.

Perhaps, in your early moments of considering what about the world you wanted to change, you thought that your company, church, team, school, neighborhood, city, or state might be impacted by your actions. I would not recommend stepping out front with that small a purpose. All of these subdivisions of people are temporary and can dissolve at any time. Even groups as large as nations sometimes disappear. To build a team that can truly create change, think bigger. Find a purpose that impacts everyone. Then enlist everyone in a cause.

Most of the ineffective leaders I have encountered over the last thirty years gathered a small team and used them as a shield. They arranged their teams around them in an attempt to prevent the realities of the world from intruding. These leaders spent all of their time handing out responsibility and accountability, while holding authority to themselves, wrongly thinking that if they controlled all of the decisions, nothing bad would happen to them. They comforted themselves with the notion that if something went wrong, one of the team members would get the blame for it. Their chief goal in life was to avoid conflict with the world. They were good at keeping things on an even keel, with as little conflict as possible. They were pursuing an agenda motivated by pain avoidance. No change was worth the risk of failure. The team only needed to hold it together for one more day.

The rest of the ineffective leaders I have observed gather a small team and use them as a shield. They arrange their team around them in an attempt to drive the team forward into the conflict. These leaders spend all of their time handing out accountability, while holding responsibility and authority for themselves, wrongly thinking if they control all decisions, they can force a victory and take all of the credit. They comfort themselves with the notion that when something goes wrong, it will happen to one of their team members. Their chief goal in life is to stay safe while driving others into conflict. They create change by shoving their team into battle, sacrificing them one by one. They are pursuing an agenda motivated by possessions and/or pride. No sacrifice is too great in accomplishing that agenda. Even the team is expendable.

Effective leaders gather a small team behind them and step out first into the conflict. There are two reasons why they do this: purpose and power. In this chapter, I want to cover the characteristics of the purpose-driven leader since they produce the most long-term improvements in the world. Power-driven leaders are effective only if they focus all of their attention on growing their power base. A large enough base can be used to leverage change by forcing the world to adjust to the large power base. These changes are seldom permanent, never productive, and typically focus on increasing the power base rather than creating improvement in the world. These are effective leaders though, because they are able to pull large teams together to back their power plays. We will look at these leaders more closely in a later chapter.

The most effective leaders that I have encountered enlist everyone. They arrange their initial small team behind them and step out first into the conflict. These leaders spend all of their time delegating authority and responsibility, while holding accountability for themselves, rightly thinking that the cause will require more decisions to be made than one person can get to. They comfort themselves with the notion that coming conflicts will hit them first and allow them to convert the combatants into team members. Their chief goal in life is to live out their purpose by promoting a cause to change the world. They have a purpose that extends beyond the current conflict, and they want everyone to come through the conflict on their team.

Often, leaders facing conflicts desire to strike out at and crush the opposition. Clean the slate. Start fresh with only you as the leader and no opposition. Noah came close to doing this, but even he still had his family with him. To change the world around you requires changing the behavior of all the people in it. Your team will need to be much larger than you thought at first.

You chose to lead when you identified something about the world that you wanted to change. When you encounter ineffective leaders who like the world the way it is, you should be able to easily convert their teams and add them to your own. Take care to know your people as you add these team members. There will be some scorners among them. With retraining, even an ineffective leader can be enlisted. When possible, peaceably defend your cause as you encounter resistance. Enlist their participation on your team by treating them the way you did the king but be ready to fight if they should resist.

From your position out front, you will encounter some effective leaders as well. Whenever possible, avoid conflict with them. Find ways to work with effective leaders. Effective leaders typically act as wise people, and you will not find any foolish or simpletons among them. Populate your team with them, and you will find growing your team much easier. Join their team if your purposes align and encourage them to join yours.

Other leaders may not be a threat, but effective leaders whose purpose is in opposition to yours should be taken seriously. Occasionally, those you are in opposition with are scorners who have managed to pull together a small following by using anarchy as a cause. They choose as their purpose the abolishment of authority, which will eventually destroy their own. These scorners are not wise and can be ignored. Some effective leaders make the acquisition of power their only purpose, and they do not always come to the same conclusions about change that you do. They may support you if doing so grows their power base, but their purpose is opposed to yours. Because these dangerous encounters can potentially play out on the world stage, often involving global armed conflict, avoiding these leaders is the best course of action. Avoidance is often not possible, so we will cover how to handle them in a later chapter.

Can the president of the PTA potentially start World War III? If your purpose was only to change the way the association communicates to parents and teachers, then your purpose is too small. I counseled against such a small purpose because it is limited enough in scope to make you and your team vulnerable to effective leaders with a larger purpose. Conflict is inevitable, and only a purpose that is larger than a single cause can sustain a leader through the coming battles, especially if the battles eventually reach the world stage. With a large purpose in mind, simply enlist everyone and press on.

Remember your purpose phrase and boldly step onto the field of conflict first. Teams follow leaders, not the other way round. Working toward an agenda blunts the impact of any cause. A purpose-driven cause defended from a physical position out front provides opportunities to grow your team. Large teams make more decisions and increase the likelihood of changing the world. Get out front to lead.

A CHALLENGE

And the Philistine said unto David, Am I a dog, that thou comest to me with staves? And the Philistine cursed David by his gods. And the Philistine said to David, Come to me, and I will give thy flesh unto the fowls of the air, and to the beasts of the field. (1 Samuel 17:43–44)

Did you ever wonder what makes politicians say such outlandish things about their political opponents? Especially in the United States and other bicameral government bodies, mudslinging seems a part of how governments create change. Watch closely though and see how little change is happening. The politicians are caught in that fifty-fifty choice that we discussed earlier. Neither side presents a compelling, obviously best plan. Debating the relative merits only creates a 50 percent chance of success in swaying enough votes. If debate is too uncertain, attacking and discrediting your opponent might help. This leaves politicians constantly struggling to outdo their opponents in mudslinging. So, they engage in issuing challenges like Goliath's and exchanging outlandish accusations in hopes of retaining the balance, not creating change.

On this battlefield in the valley of Elah, we see two diametrically opposed groups. Both have accepted that complete victory is the only desired outcome, but they are also so committed to the world as it is that neither side is likely to take action to create that victory. Goliath has created a distraction for the armies by presenting himself as the single point of resistance and insisting that Israel must send only one champion to face him. The seemingly obvious outcome of that fight ensures that no one will step out to fight. This creates a standoff similar to the balance of power in a bicameral body, and no one wants to risk upsetting the balance because they fear the outcome of the coin toss.

Goliath participates in the time-honored tradition of insulting his opponent, cursing his existence, and inviting him to a physical conflict that will result in an obvious outcome. When you encounter resistance, expect the same sort of challenge. The insult and the curse will be personal but have no bearing on your purpose, so ignore them. Focus on the consequences of conflict that are described and refuse to be afraid. Your opponent will use the description of consequences to make your team afraid. By refusing fear, you remove that negative motivation and free your team to allow the cause to be their only motivation in this conflict.

The leader you are confronting on your battlefield will have something similar to say. They have worked hard to produce the world as they know it and are determined to keep it that way. Conflict is not what they want; they want stability. Fear generated by the threat of conflict maintains the balance. Refuse to be afraid. Your purpose is to create a change, your cause has been accepted by the king, and your team is ready to follow, so tell them what you are going to do.

SIMPLE PLAN

Remember from chapter 1 that the vision is the clearly defined outcome that the leader is attempting to accomplish. While the leader's determination implants and keeps the vision continually in the team's collective thinking, this action by the leader only creates buy-in from the team. They must accept the vision as their personal goal. Only when the entire team sees and seeks to accomplish the vision can it be manufactured. The team makes it happen, not the leader. The vision is only the starting point.

David's purpose to please God by accomplishing the cause of removing the Philistines as a reproach has gotten him this far. David is out front and has received Goliath's challenge. Goliath has not repented and removed the reproach. All David needs now is an army to remove that reproach. In fact, he will need two armies. David wants to enlist the Israeli army to attack and the Philistine army to run. Before entering into battle against Goliath, he presents a vision designed to motivate both armies to action.

Then said David to the Philistine, Thou comest to me with a sword, and with a spear, and with a shield: but I come to thee in the name of the LORD of hosts, the God of the armies of Israel, whom thou hast defied. This day will the LORD deliver thee into mine hand; and I will smite thee, and take thine head from thee; and I will give the carcases of the host of the Philistines this day unto the fowls of the air, and to the wild beasts of the earth; that all the earth may know that there is a God in Israel. And all this assembly shall know that the LORD saveth not with sword and spear: for the battle is the LORD'S, and he will give you into our hands. (1 Samuel 17: 45–47)

Effective leaders do not run from conflict; they encourage their teams to follow them into it. David draws attention to the need for conflict by pointing to the weapons that Goliath is carrying. Goliath used these weapons to create fear, which kept the Israeli army from acting. David draws attention to them but without fear. Then he provides his team with a reason for his fearlessness. David's purpose makes him bold, or more directly, the God who gives focus to his purpose. David offers the army a chance to take up his purpose to be a man after God's own heart, fearlessly moving forward to accomplish His objectives.

This is as close as David comes to defining his purpose for everyone to see. His purpose gives him a clear picture of the real battle. This is not a contest between two armies but rather a contest between the Philistines and God. Throughout their history, Israel has always triumphed over superior enemies, not because of their superior battle skills but because God designed that they should win. David reminds Israel that this has always worked out for them in the past, and he reminds the Philistines that those who have opposed the armies of Israel have typically been defeated. Goliath has massive weapons of war at his disposal, but in a conflict against God, those weapons are of no use. David's purpose allows him to clearly articulate the reversal of fear in a single sentence.

Your team needs to know enough of your purpose to be able to see the past proofs that support this cause, and your opponents need a compelling reason to change. Both need to see that success is possible if everyone plays their part. There can be no half-hearted commitment here. Your purpose must be an integrated part of your life, and the cause should produce significant change in accord with that purpose. Show your team the improvements that will come with action, and they will follow.

David follows the proof with a deadline and repeats it for emphasis. Considering how tired and trying a day he has had, waiting until tomorrow would have been understandable. The journey by foot from Bethlehem to the valley of Elah took half the day already. Then he had to raise a cause, confront his brother, convince the king, walk past the safety of the front lines, and find Goliath. He turned the tables on the fear equation in the valley and could rightly have taken a break for dinner and a good night's rest. But the armies were in array and ready for battle. All they needed to know was when the battle was to take place. He could have waited until tomorrow, but deadlines prompt actions.

After going through all the effort necessary to reach this point in your leadership path, do not slow down to rest. Set a short deadline first for what you will do, then for what your team will do. Many leaders fail at this point simply because they are too tired to take immediate action. There will be time for rest later. Resting now will only allow circumstances to change and the window of opportunity to close. As the leader, you must set the deadline for completion, move forward immediately, and take action.

When I received that delegation to replace the embezzling manager, I had some additional small changes I thought should be made. The team I supervised wanted to know how their work lives would be improved by having me as their leader, and I had no vision for them. When I tried to make the small changes I had in mind, the conflicts began, and without a purpose to drive me forward to lead my team through the conflict, they began leaving. Soon, I left too.

I was freshly out of the navy and just beginning my studies in leadership. I had not developed a purpose, and work was just an interesting way to pass the time and pay the bills. Creating a business that makes sense was fun, so I found small processes that could be improved, which fulfilled my own pride motivators but left my team with no real direction. They were ready to make the world a better place, and I wanted to change the message on our outgoing faxes. With no cause to pursue, the team was left to the daily grind. Like the Israeli army, they suited up daily and went to the field of battle expecting nothing more to happen. All they needed from me was a vision and a deadline.

Publicly announce a simple plan where you as the leader take the first action and provide a short timeline for completion. The public announcement is the only way to enlist everyone. It also commits the leader to a single course of action, eliminating ambiguity. Change is imminent, and everyone now knows it. The balance that has held everyone in stasis can now be broken with one act from the leader. Leaders must act. Teams accomplish the cause, but their actions follow the leader's actions. With a team at the ready, the leader needs only to succeed in the announced action, and the team will take over. The short timeline curbs further debate because there is no time. Action is all that is left for everyone.

TIME TO ACT

All leaders eventually need to act. Breaking the balance of opinion and fear requires action. Purpose creates cause; cause wins authority; authority comes with responsibility; and responsibility requires action. Demonstrably, the precepts and concepts of leadership are an integrated whole. If pressed to identify a single secret of success as a leader, I would point to the precept that leaders must act first. Discourse and debate are a part of politics in bicameral systems, but these activities have never solved a single problem and will never bring change. Action creates change.

Planning happens in chapters 1 through 5. Choose to lead by creating change. Find something that needs to change. Define a purpose to provide proper motivation. Create a cause to gain authority. Gather your tools and create a rapid response methodology (OODA). Act now!

PRECEPTS

- Get out front.
- Enlist everyone.
- Deadlines prompt actions.
- Leaders act first.

7

———◆———

MANAGED RISK

I f Samuel were a scriptwriter for Hollywood, the battle scene would build slowly from here to the climax. The prologue of the story of David and Goliath contains conflict and drama, leading us to believe the battle sequence will be full of moves within moves, attacks, and counterattacks, culminating in the release of David's superhero power that turns the tide. Then one more exchange between our hero and the giant allows a final opportunity for repentance. Goliath would die coughing and spitting curses. End scene.

Samuel does not appear to have been overly impressed with the actual battle nor interested in making a superhero movie. He wrote two sentences. Halfway through the second sentence, the rock strikes Goliath's forehead. Samuel's simple recounting reads like eyewitness testimony, not a movie. He provides simple facts to convey the action, with no embellishment.

And it came to pass, when the Philistine arose, and came and drew nigh to meet David, that David hasted, and ran toward the army to meet the Philistine. And David put his hand in his bag, and took thence a stone, and slang it, and smote the Philistine in his forehead, that the stone sunk into his forehead; and he fell upon his face to the earth. (1 Samuel 17:48, 49)

David's battle plan is simple: trust that God will remove the reproach, run behind Goliath where there is no shield, stay out of reach, and throw rocks at his opponent. Goliath moves forward to attack, but he is weighed down by heavy armor and is behind a massive shield that cannot be moved quickly. David runs toward the army to meet the Philistine. If he is running to meet Goliath, then he is running toward the Philistine army and away from the safety of his countrymen. David moves quickly to get behind the shield. Goliath's size and the weight of his armor slow him down enough that David has time to launch a rock at his head. A simple plan, well executed, leading to the desired outcome, but there is significant risk involved.

In a superhero movie, we sit and watch with calm assurance that the good guy will win in the end, but David is not a superhero; he is a shepherd. During the time he was preparing and gathering the stones, he would have had time to consider the risks. He might have been able to adjust his plan to remove or to mitigate those risks, but once he ran toward the army, he could then only encounter the risks as they came. Running toward the opposing army removed all possibility of escape. David was fully committed to his purpose and to this battle. He embraced the risk.

Pursue any cause long enough, and eventually, you arrive in the same place as David, with everything on the line and no option except to fight. When you find yourself out front on the battlefield, having just announced your plan to everyone and you are now acting, be bold, be deliberate, leaving no way out except victory. David's battle plan moved him fully into the conflict with no escape routes. He is now closer to the Philistine army, farther from the Israeli army, and has an angry giant between himself and safety. When your moment arrives, hold nothing back, step forward, and embrace the risk.

We do not know what David was thinking when he collected more than one stone, but we can see from his actions that he was giving himself the best chance of success in the battle. David's plan was risky. In fact, watching from a distance, we might have expected that the small, unarmed combatant was most likely to be destroyed. He could have spent more time assessing the risks, but the decision point would be the same, and he would have to embrace the risk.

RISK

Your team will not fully commit unless they see that you have already done so. They will follow, but you will have to be in front showing them where to go and how to get there. Risk inherently exists in any battle or conflict. If your cause is to be won, your actions need to demonstrate to your team that you have embraced the risk.

Risk is the possibility that harm, damage, or loss will result from a course of action. Risks are most often categorized by their severity if realized and the probability of their being encountered. The size or amount of loss is often the easiest to assess. Calculating the probability of a given risk is more complicated because of the future's lack of predictability. We can never know for certain what will happen in the future; we can only give our best guess. Assigning a number between 0 percent and 100 percent can be done with a calculator and advanced actuarial math, or with a blindfold and a dart. As a leader, your best guess, based on intuition, may be all you have time for. Regardless of the calculated number, you will have to embrace the risk if you want to advance your cause.

If time permits, some risk can be managed so that the estimates seem more favorable. For instance, David could have spent a half hour practicing with his sling and warming up his muscles prior to entering the battlefield. This preparation might have identified loose knots on the sling or prepared his muscles to move a slight bit faster, and either could have improved his chances of success. Those improved changes are still not a guarantee. Risk will always exist when entering the battle, and embracing that risk is the best strategy for overcoming it.

This moment is not only about the risks you are embracing but also your team's exposure to risk. The risks you embrace will affect everyone, so take the time necessary to find conviction before assuming risk. For David, the proposition that was offered by Goliath would end with the Israelites being enslaved to the Philistines if he should fail. Your team will face dire consequences if you fail, so be certain that you embrace necessary risks.

If realized, each risk will have both a positive and a negative impact. Because you are attempting to change the world, positive results for you are negative results for those who like the world as it is. Remember that one of your precepts is to enlist everyone, and though they may not like the changes you are proposing, they will need to adjust to those changes or be removed from the equation. Being a leader is a zero-sum game where your gain will be someone else's loss.

Assessing the risks begins with identification of what is possible. As David engages with Goliath, these are the possible outcomes I see:

1. Goliath loses and is killed.
2. David loses and is killed.
3. Both combatants are injured so that neither can fight on.

These are of course the recognizable possible outcomes.

Any number of unrecognizable risks also exists, such as another army joining the fight that morning. An earthquake, swarm of bees, or flood could have interfered at the exact moment that David entered the battle. But considering any of these unrecognizable events would be a waste of time. Donning a beekeeper's baggy clothes and netting to prevent the possibility of bee stings would not be a productive use of time before entering a battle with a giant. In short, all unrecognizable risks must be embraced without any management effort.

Imagine you are the captain of the SS *Min Now*. After twenty years of life at sea, you have developed a highly refined understanding of the weather and its effects on the sea. One day while taking a group of tourists on an excursion cruise around your home island, you notice a storm on the horizon. Its size, location, and time of day are familiar, and you have sailed safely around such storms many times in the past. One obvious, recognizable risk stands out. The storm might sink the *Min Now*, which is the most significant risk to all on board.

By applying all of the advanced mathematical theories imaginable concerning weather, wave motion, engine power, hull design, and sports handicapping, you might calculate the likelihood or probability of sinking at 30 percent, after several hours of calculations. You as captain must decide now, without the time for calculations, and your probability estimation may be nothing more than "better than average." The result is the same either way; you sail on past the point of no return, confident that the *Min Now* will not sink. Unfortunately, you never considered that the ship would be damaged, stranding you and your passengers on a deserted island.

This is the nature of assessing risk. No matter how observant, open-minded, or experienced you are, not all risks will be identified. Using advanced statistics (calculation) or your years of experience (intuition) produce the same result for the risks you do recognize. When time and data exist, calculation always provides the most comfort. Intuition is quick and can often produce the same decisions. Both methods have pitfalls. Neither predicts the future. So, either way, you will have to embrace the risk.

Calculation

Done effectively, calculations provide a level of confidence that actions will result in the desired outcome, but that confidence may be misplaced. The field of statistics provides a mathematical formula that is called a confidence interval. Calculating a confidence interval is easy enough to do with a calculator and a few simple inputs. Understanding those inputs does require some moderate math skills, but a high school education is usually sufficient for a basic calculation. Study the confidence interval online if you would like a simple method of calculation that can be applied to risk assessment. Notice as you study that the discussion about the interval always describes the result as an estimate. Even when enormous amounts of sample data are available, the future remains unpredictable. Consider carefully though that being 90 percent confident that an event will occur in the future is the same as being 10 percent confident that it will not. Confidence is not the same as certainty.

Assumption and bias remain ever-present detractors in these calculations. Not all data needed for an accurate prediction can be discovered. Some assumptions are always made, which creates the "interval" part of the confidence interval. The interval is a range of outcomes based on the uncertainty of the assumptions made. With only a little practice and moderate math skills, any leader can easily change an interval by choosing different assumptions. Once the pattern is recognized, the calculations become unstable because the leader can now choose to change the interval in favor of the desired outcome. This bias to choose assumptions that push the result in favor of the leader's chosen course is why this form of estimation is best done by an outside observer, since their assumptions are less likely to be biased to a specific outcome.

Because the interval can be adjusted by assumptions and bias, choosing the least number of assumptions may seem preferable. The practice of preferring the simplest models is often referred to as the principle of Occam's Razor. This notion that the simplest model is the most likely to be true can be supported by logic, but the math does not always prove this to be true. Often, the more complex model contains a more accurate representation of the probable outcomes. In the end, missing even one assumption, such as the likelihood of damage that does not sink the ship, spoils the result of any confidence interval. Simple or multivariate estimations of future events are only guesses. They should never be considered predictions.

Calculation's most glaring pitfall is the assignment of a risk estimate based on the gambler's fallacy. This is an extreme example of how the number of assumptions or the bias that chooses the assumptions can impact the outcome of decisions. If a six-chambered pistol holds one bullet, our assessment of risk might tell us that we have a 17 percent chance of firing a shot on the first pull of the trigger. The second chamber has a probability of 20 percent, the third 25 percent, continuing until the fifth shot when the probability is 50 percent. If a gambler were offered $1B for each time he raised the gun to his head and pulled the trigger, how many chambers would be clicked on before he stops? Even an aggressive gambler would not go any further than four, not daring the fifty-fifty chance on the fifth chamber.

For this fantasy to work, on the first trigger pull, our gambler borrows the remaining chambers to give a false sense of confidence. While there is certainly a 17 percent chance that the first chamber has the bullet, making the decision to pull the trigger eliminates the other five chambers from consideration. After the trigger pulls, the gun will fire or it will not, based on only that one chamber. To gain the confidence to pull the trigger, the gambler reaches into the future attempting to predict which chamber has the bullet. His bias for the desired outcome forces him to assume that one of the other chambers is equally likely to hold the bullet. While that assumption is accurate when the pistol is inert, once that decision is reached to pull the trigger, the other chambers are no longer a part of the equation. Each time our gambler pulls the trigger, there is a 50 percent chance of disaster, which is a condition that he would not accept in the fifth chamber. His desire to gain the money might get him to use the more complex model containing all the chambers, but in this instance, the simpler model based on one chamber is at least less likely to produce disaster.

Our gambler is likely to pull the trigger and die long before collecting any reward since each pull is an either/or scenario. The large reward causes him to seek alternative calculations attempting to cheat the system and gain an advantage. Bias created by a strong possession motivator chooses unrealistic assumptions to increase confidence and create an acceptable risk assessment. The argument could be made that if the bullet were in the last chamber, we reach a 100 percent chance of disaster, but the gun could jam or the bullet misfire. I would not recommend to our gambler that he include those assumptions in his model. Nor would I recommend he expect anything other than disaster on the first trigger pull.

Bias applied to the selection of assumptions fascinates me. Over the last several weeks, my attention has been drawn to the risk calculations being conducted to predict the outcome of the COVID-19 pandemic. Each day, often several times a day, one or more politicians conduct a press conference to explain a new calculation model that demonstrates that the risk of continued spread is either increasing or decreasing. The models are simply calculations of risk. Each new model disagrees with the models presented on the previous day, and often models used by one politician disagree with models used at other press conferences by the same politician. In retrospect, none of the models accurately predicted the spread or severity of the disease, but each was presented with absolute certainty during the press conferences.

Some politicians deliberately chose differing models for consecutive press releases, saying alternately the disease is going to worsen or it is getting better, depending on the message they wanted to deliver to the press. In the early-morning release, a politician might explain a model that demonstrated clearly that the risk is being reduced because of their dedicated efforts on behalf of their constituents. The same politician that evening, during a conference to demonstrate the need for additional funding, could use a model that clearly indicates that the spread is out of control and the risk of contagion is increasing. Two days later, the same politician reverses the risk estimates to demonstrate the ineffective efforts of a rival politician. Calculations do not produce predictions of the future. They provide validation for our actions based on our bias in choosing the assumptions.

Leaders do not require calculations to make effective decisions, but calculations can provide the confidence needed to act. When the risk of confrontation in the next few minutes reaches 100 percent, and the leader needs to act, a confidence interval of 90 percent might provide the push needed to embrace the risk. Taking the time to prepare for this moment by committing fully to a purpose that is written down and rehearsed is more likely to provide the correct level of confidence to act. No intervals, estimations, assumptions, or bias are needed if the purpose is clearly defined and the leader is committed to it.

Intuition

Sometimes you just know. If you drive your new car across the arena during a demolition derby, you should expect some damage. Witnessing a demolition derby in the past, or better still, driving in one, can provide all the confidence needed to declare that damage is imminent. This sort of recognition of the likelihood of risk without the need for calculations is how most people assess risk.

Intuition works because risk is not random. Bad outcomes do not hit unexpectedly. Your actions are causes that create effects in the world around you. When the effects of your actions do not meld with the conditions of the world around you, the leaders who have created that world will take action to stop you. In David's case, his action of announcing the defeat of the Philistine army before the sun went down motivated Goliath to take action to stop him. The intrinsic risk in David's announcement was not knowing what Goliath would do next, but intuition would see the increased risk of attack.

Intuition is most successful when the leader has a plethora of experience to rely on. A veteran firefighter who has successfully entered buildings to rescue occupants is more likely to succeed in the endeavor next time. But the rookie who is younger, in better physical condition, but lacking the same number of positive outcomes might have the same intuitive risk assessment as the veteran. This is one of the reasons why leaders should depend on those actions that are familiar and well-practiced. The veteran has experience, and the rookie has preparation and strength, so that both come to the same conclusion of expectant success in a rescue attempt.

For David, he has had success in the past, taking actions that were dependent on the skills he had been practicing as a shepherd: move fast and use your sling to eliminate threats. Had he followed Saul's plan, he might have drawn a sword and charged at Goliath with a mighty swing, only to encounter the tip of Goliath's spear. Use intuition to assess the risks of familiar actions for the best success.

Not all situations that a leader faces will have familiar elements. Intuition works best with some degree of familiarity. Effective leaders often rely on another person's experience to provide an intuitive assessment of risk. Deferring to the advice of experts can be useful in assessing risks through intuition but take care. You will be accountable for the decisions made by this expert, so be certain you understand their motivation. Bias chosen to support that expert's desired outcome of advancing their career might lead you into the middle of the derby without a car. Be certain you know your people if you plan to use their intuition.

Managing Risk

Risk arises from the inability to predict the future. No amount of circumspection can ever reveal all the risks of a chosen course of action. Since risk exists in any action, leaders who want to make progress on a cause often seek ways to manage the risk. Managing the risk would involve altering the plan or conditions of conflict to either eliminate, reduce the likelihood of, or reduce the effects of risks. I discovered over the years that we have three basic strategies for managing risk: mitigation, avoidance, and rejection. My exploration of each of these strategies produced a mixed bag of good and bad results.

Mitigation

In my early days of leadership study, risk mitigation was my strategy of choice. Mitigation is acting to either reduce the likelihood or severity of the consequences of recognized risks. With mitigation, I would evaluate the most likely risk, then adjust my team or circumstances to reduce the likelihood or at least reduce the severity of those risks. These mitigation efforts only reduced the possibility of the risk but never removed it entirely.

Mitigation efforts consume enormous amounts of time and resources, often on risks that will never materialize. My most wasted efforts were spent trying to eliminate the risk entirely. Typically, these mitigation efforts only increase the likelihood of other risks. If these were realized, the mitigation efforts might serve to refocus the likelihood on the originally mitigated risk. Either way, my teams never had a leader's actions to follow, so that by the time I acted, I no longer had their support.

All potential risks might happen, and I never had enough time to mitigate them all. Attempting to identify and reduce the likelihood or impact of every risk is a fool's errand. I discovered that only the risks with the greatest potential danger or those with the highest probability of realization should be mitigated, and mitigation efforts should reduce the severity of the consequences. At least those mitigation efforts were not likely to be wasted and might allow my team to hold together through the risk event.

As you sail the *Min Now* into the storm, as a good captain, you would take the time to batten down the hatches, secure everything on the deck, and at least pass out flotation vests to your passengers. This type of mitigation can also provide mitigating effects on unrecognized risks. For your passengers, they will have the best chance of making it to shore in the storm if they have on their flotation vests. For David, taking five stones instead of one would leave him prepared for many recognized and unrecognized risks.

The future cannot be predicted, so the risks it contains should be confronted and the results mitigated. I learned to spend present effort on decisions leading to manageable risk rather than mitigating all risks. I take action to mitigate the damage of the most prominent risks and then embrace the rest.

Avoidance

For a short season, I practiced risk avoidance by choosing decisions more carefully. Instead of attempting to mitigate bad outcomes, I searched for optimal decisions that had no bad outcomes. This is the often-touted act of looking for a win-win scenario, but changing the world means that someone will lose. Any cause worth pursuing will eventually end in a zero-sum event where someone wins, and someone loses. Risk cannot be avoided because conflict cannot be avoided if change happens.

In avoiding risk, I realized that I was following the lead of those who had established the world as it is. This is not always a bad strategy, because aligning yourself to the world as it is provides a higher degree of confidence in success. Changing the world this way is not only impossible, but any decision to create change will bring you into conflict. Any strong leader who creates change will destroy all those win-wins that the world is built on.

Avoidance most often leads to inaction though. While decisions should not be made until they must be made, avoidance behavior often takes a leader past the deadline. These leaders are convinced that they still need more information and continue orienting past the time for action. Teams that are sitting idle past the deadline will eventually find another leader to follow.

Rejection

Another strategy that I am embarrassed to admit using is rejection. This strategy involves rejecting the notion that risk exists and making decisions that attempt to force the outcome I want. Like the gambler letting it ride on one roll of the dice or turn of a card, I abandoned all circumspection in favor of an immediate decision and action.

Running this rejection gamble is the antithesis of the gambler's fallacy because it does not attempt to predict the future but force it. I discovered that these gambles were most often attempting to force agendas rather than advance a cause. I learned the hard way that risk is real and cannot be rejected. Yes, it would be amazing to watch a video of someone putting on a blindfold and then driving their new car across the arena at a demolition derby, managing to reach the other side with no damage. But your team deserves better than to be riding in the back seat while you try to star in that video.

EMBRACE THE RISK

Assuming risk is the only real option. Mitigation is rational, but those efforts do not eliminate the risk. Avoidance moves a leader away from the conflict and away from the cause. Rejecting the existence of the risk results in a leader being blindsided. Since risk cannot be managed, it must be embraced. The leader will have to enter the conflict and work moment to moment to prevent bad outcomes. Familiar actions, using familiar tools in conflicts where risk has been mitigated provide the best possibility of success, but the risks must be embraced to create change.

Be ready when you embrace risk to have it sometimes realized. David was prepared to throw more than one stone but not more than five. If he missed that many times of course, Goliath would have turned around, gotten his shield in place, and closed the distance to David. David could have run around him again, found some more stones, and continued the battle. For David, that was a risk he was willing to embrace, for the possibility of accomplishing the cause that was empowered by his purpose.

David had less than a day between choosing the cause and embracing the risk. Hopefully in your efforts to lead, you have more time than David. Your purpose may have some inherent risks that you can mitigate and be ready to embrace far in advance of choosing a cause. The cause will introduce additional risks that can be mitigated while you are gaining authority. When the vision is announced, your deadline will introduce more risk but may provide some time for mitigation. At each step along the way, mitigate what you can, but then be ready to embrace all those risks now.

David slung a stone and struck Goliath in the forehead. Samuel conveys this battle to us in two sentences. David acted simply, with tools and skills that were familiar, to mitigate the risks, but the risks were still there. He could easily have tripped on a rock while running, missed with the first stone, or broken his sling. A bear could have stepped out of the woods and eaten him. All these risks had to be embraced for David to gain victory.

PRECEPTS

- Embrace the risk.

8

---◀ ● ▶---

FINISH

Failed leadership often results from a lack of mental preparation for success. Our examination of risk likely resonated with your experiences because as humans we spend an inordinate amount of time preparing for the worst-case scenarios. Risk assessments and management strategies are characteristic tools in our daily lives as we adjust our thinking and emotional framework to get ready for the next tragedy that will come. Before we reach adulthood, each of us experiences enough tragedy to last for a lifetime, and we develop strategies for coping. Reducing the pain of the next tragedy becomes pathological in our preparation for tomorrow, but seldom do we prepare for success.

The precepts in this book and the framework that they create increases the probability of success. While tragedy is still possible, the more likely outcome of a disciplined approach to leadership rooted in an articulated purpose is success. If tragedy is all that the leader is prepared to encounter, any success can easily derail a cause. A leader who is suddenly confronted with success and who has not prepared for it may freeze, but the accomplishment of only one small part of the announced vision will not get the team moving. The leader must prepare for success and be ready to finish the job.

Therefore, effective leaders think about and prepare for success. Preparing for success is a precept that may seem to have its origins in the modern ideas of positive thinking but reading the description of the wise man in proverbs demonstrates a clear picture that wise actions produce successful results. Wishful, positive thinking lifts moods but produces no net positive effect on a cause beyond that. Following a disciplined approach to accomplishing a cause has a high probability of success, so a wise leader will spend time preparing for that first successful step to know in advance what they will do next.

David's preparation was built into his battle plan, the one he announced to the two armies. David promised to kill Goliath. Done! Both armies stood on their respective mountains, watching to see what would happen next on the valley floor. Goliath fell to the ground after being hit with a stone, but no one was convinced that Goliath was dead. David promised to take his head from him, and the armies were waiting to see that happen. According to Samuel's description, David was prepared to deal with his success by having the next step in mind. He knew he had to take Goliath's head to finish the job.

So David prevailed over the Philistine with a sling and with a stone, and smote the Philistine, and slew him; but there was no sword in the hand of David. Therefore David ran, and stood upon the Philistine, and took his sword, and drew it out of the sheath thereof, and slew him, and cut off his head therewith. And when the Philistines saw their champion was dead, they fled. (1 Samuel 17:50–51)

Preparing for success does not always mean that the leader has laid out an exact path to finish the job. Plans are good preparation items that seldom hold together past the first contact with the world. Finishing the job starts with the right perspective on the conditions that define a finished job. David's purpose grew to a cause that led to authority that allowed for action that killed a giant, but the stated cause was to remove a reproach against God. The Philistine army still stood on the other mountain in opposition to Israel. David killed Goliath but had not removed the reproach of the army.

In parallel with our earlier discussion about using what you know, this is another time to fall back on that precept. David's initial plans were made with a giant standing in his way. The situation has now changed. The risk profile shifted, and both armies are now free from stalemate. Israel finds hope in the prone giant, and the Philistine army finds fear. But is he dead or just down? David's next action is to run to Goliath. As with the bear and the lion that formed the basis of David's proof for the king, he knows to get up close and personal with the enemy if he wants to deliver the lamb from its mouth and finish the job.

And David said unto Saul, Thy servant kept his father's sheep, and there came a lion, and a bear, and took a lamb out of the flock: And I went out after him, and smote him, and delivered it out of his mouth: and when he arose against me, I caught him by his beard, and smote him, and slew him. (1 Samuel 17:34, 35)

So David prevailed over the Philistine with a sling and with a stone, and smote the Philistine, and slew him; but there was no sword in the hand of David. Therefore David ran, and stood upon the Philistine, and took his sword, and drew it out of the sheath thereof, and slew him, and cut off his head therewith. And when the Philistines saw their champion was dead, they fled. (1 Samuel 17:50, 51)

In the past, David delivered the lamb only to discover that the thief was not yet dead and still had some fight left. Lion, bear, or giant, the pattern of actions is the same. David does not look for or implement a new battle strategy because of the uniqueness of the situation. Rather, he relies on proven tactics that he has learned while doing the work he was assigned. As a leader, when you are called upon to accomplish the impossible, simply do what you already know how to do. And do it until you finish the job.

Getting the armies moving will require David to act again to demonstrate victory completely by following through to finish the job by removing Goliath's head. Be careful what you communicate during your vision announcement because the people whose lives you are trying to change will hold you to the exact words of your promised actions. If you do not have the stomach, skills, or will to complete the announced actions, your cause will only come close to fruition. Completing the cause requires the completion of the leader's announced actions.

Finishing a job changes the world and the leader. The leader changes most. The level of responsibility assumed is proportional to the number of people who will now be following your lead. As the change propagates into the world, many more people will join your team who were positively impacted by your actions. Even those who see the change as a negative will have to accommodate you now that the change has happened. Like baptism, the leader emerges as a different person. David was a man after God's own heart, but God does not allow David to build the first temple because this moment of success against a giant altered him and made him into a man of blood. Your change may not be as dramatic but finishing the job will change who you are.

David may have considered how his next action would change him, or he may have acted simply because he promised to do so. Samuel had no way of knowing what David was thinking, but he does tell us that David acted without hesitation. He moved to complete the task even though he was not fully equipped. He ran to where Goliath fell and only after he got there decided how to accomplish the task at hand. The same way he went out to catch the lion and the bear, he ran to finish the job of removing the reproach by next removing Goliath's head.

These two precepts, prepare for success and finish the job, are intricately linked. When success comes, a leader can easily be overwhelmed with pride and forget the promises that were made. Those promises were made explicitly in the vision statement, and the team will not act until those promises are kept. Many leaders pause here to enjoy a well-deserved pat on the back, but if the vision was clear and had a deadline, there is no time for delay. Preparing for success is the only way to be ready to finish the job.

PREPARE FOR SUCCESS

Finishing the job begins with preparing for success. For me, being prepared for success requires dealing with three aspects of human nature where we all fall short: pride, promises, and panic. Immediately following a successful action, pride can inflate beyond a leader's capacity to manage and overwhelm the purposeful motivation that led to success. Preparing to short-circuit that pride helps a leader focus on the next required action for progress on the stated cause. The announced vision always contains a form of proof that was not mentioned in chapter 4 because it is too weak to gain a king's authority—a promise. Making a promise will not get a king's attention but keeping a promise will get the team's attention. Beware of panic. It is more dangerous than the giant was, and now that the giant is down, panic can overwhelm the unprepared.

Pride

In chapter 3, we examined how to use pride as a motivational influence for your team members. Understanding how pride can affect your team's actions should give you some perspective of the complications you will face when experiencing success. As soon as success hits, pride will well up. Pride of person inflates because you acted according to your ideal and won a victory. Suddenly your place out front is a source of pride rather than a commitment to lead, and your delegation from the king is now a cherished possession instead of an obligation. Working to foster any of these pride ideas draws attention from your purpose, leaving your cause unfinished.

This is a tricky moment for any leader when pride can take over. Pride can be a powerful motivational force that helps a leader overcome fear. When the actions are consistent with the announced vision to accomplish a cause, the leader can expect continued success. Pride can be used by a leader as a motivator to move toward the vision's accomplishment, but it can easily overwhelm the most well-intentioned leader. Preventing pride from replacing purpose requires deliberate moderation.

Accomplishing the first action on the path to winning a team's involvement is a moment that should produce pride. Effective leaders deliberately manage the impact of that pride. Wise leaders build a short circuit into their vision that prevents pride from taking over their purpose. A planned short circuit is an important step in preparing for success. In all of my observations of leaders, I have discovered three methods that are commonly deployed as short circuits for pride: luck, loss prevention, and largesse. The first two lead to ruin, and the third continued success.

Luck

One strategy to short-circuit pride is to attribute success to luck. First, decide if you are lucky. Dirty Harry stared over the sites of his .44 Super Mag. to ask the criminal he was chasing this same question. Any leader arriving at a crossroads where the next choice leads to world change or failure will at least implicitly consider the events of their life before proceeding. If the leader perceives themselves as lucky, they embrace elevated levels of risk, while unlucky leaders avoid or deny risk.

The concept of luck originates in the assigning of positive or negative labels to random events. Returning to the gambler's fallacy mentioned earlier, a leader begins to see patterns that tip the scale toward recognition of more positive or more negative outcomes. Most people tend to identify trends in these labels over time that determine if they are lucky or unlucky.

Either conclusion is dangerous because both originate in a perception of a pattern where one does not exist. Disciplined actions create a pattern of success, and undisciplined actions create a pattern of chaos. Discipline, and not luck, predicts success.

Remember from an earlier chapter that successful leadership is a zero-sum game, and most of the people affected by a change are going to see it as a negative because it changed the world, they were comfortable with. Changes in the world are both good and bad, depending on perspective. Outcomes are both positive and negative. Which group a person belongs to, the world that was changed, or the team that changed it determines the appropriate label. The pattern established by the frequency of the attached labels defines the effectiveness of the leaders that created the changes, not luck.

Acceptance of a proper cause and effect relationship between actions and outcomes provides a clearer picture of the truth about luck. A leader must first accept the premise that no random events take place. All events are effects that can be attached to causes. From that starting point, a leader predicts outcomes based on chosen actions. The outcomes develop from the leader's actions, not as a result of the leader's level of luck.

The proposed change can be positive and still have negative consequences for the leader. As mentioned earlier, David's success will cause Saul to put a price on his head. A leader who is dedicated to challenging risk because they feel lucky is headed for disaster if negative outcomes flow from success. Success in the cause is the positive outcome that is desired, and the unintended consequences are unrecognized risks that must be embraced. Assuming that some fantasy force of nature called luck turns the tide in the leader's favor leads to ruin, not fortune.

Claiming that random chance creates success is disingenuous at best since success is the conclusion of a series of right actions. Trying to tell yourself that you were just lucky is not likely to stop the pride that you deserve to feel. My grandfather was fond of saying, "There is no such thing as luck. It's just clean living." Doing the right thing and getting a good result is by definition not lucky. As the leader, you are out front where everyone wants to be, you have acted independently, and you have moved toward your purpose by accomplishing your first announced action. While others on the sidelines might see this as lucky, the leader knows better. Since luck cannot have any meaningful impact on success, I do not recommend leaning on it as a way to short-circuit pride.

Loss Prevention

Some leaders will announce a failure state to be avoided in their vision statement. Preventing the possible loss is given equal footing with the cause. David could have started his challenge to Goliath by saying, "In order to avoid Israel becoming slaves to the Philistines ..." The failure state could be in the past, present, or future and will represent a significant amount of loss if realized. Preventing the loss grows in importance until it replaces purpose.

Tragedy fills the better part of our lives. Planning for it easily becomes the focus of even a well-intentioned leader. Tragedies are events that a person perceives as negative, that are either random in nature, unintended consequences of pursuing a cause, or consequences of a change in the world created by another leader. Lightning striking the ground and starting a fire is tragic but not directed. Becoming the enemy of the king who delegated the authority to act is a probable outcome of pursuing a cause but seldom anticipated. Anyone can exercise leadership, and other leaders may be creating changes to the world that you experience as being negative and perhaps even tragic. Setting out on a path of pain avoidance ensures that avoiding these tragedies replaces purpose.

Leaders codify tragedy through years of careful analysis. These tragic events get recast as a collection of conditions that led to a failure state. Because the conditions predate the tragedy, leaders learn to see them as predictive even without causal ties. These conditions become the proverbial black cat. The leader's focus shifts from purpose to preventing loss by creating rules that eliminate the conditions that appear to cause tragedy. Fear now dominates the motivational spectrum for the leader, and the rules that prevent the loss grow in importance.

Leading with fear instead of a cause derives tyranny. Tyranny is achieved when the leader dictates a singular perspective based on loss prevention. The leader requires all team members to participate in avoiding the conditions that led to failure. Everyone must follow the rules. Tyrants never encounter a time when the probability of tragedy is eliminated. Rules become magic talismans that create safety for the team. The codified conditions of failure are relevant to the leader and are seldom articulated to the team because they could then be used as weapons by any rebels in the group. Loss prevention supplants purpose, becoming pathologically dogmatic with continued success until avoidance is the cause and purpose that drives the leader. The team goes along for the ride as they work feverishly to prevent the leader's secretive and irrational failure conditions.

The tyrant is always deposed by their team. Insisting that a group of people pursue an irrational goal will require significant and oft-repeated threats of violence. Violence against a single rebellious team member puts down initial rebellions. The level and frequency of violence escalate until it precipitates a more violent backlash from a majority of the team that ends with the effective destruction of the tyrannical leader.

Tyrannical leadership is not always destructive to the team but is always devoid of purposeful intent and therefore destructive to the leader who accomplishes it. In chapter 10, we will examine the power-driven model of leadership, which is always tyrannical. Team members are seduced into joining and then trapped by their desire to find safety and security from the majority of the world. Joining the team is a compromise where the team member is protected from the world by becoming completely vulnerable to the leader's capriciousness. While the team may grow, they will have no cause to accomplish and will eventually rebel.

Learning to be a tyrant is seldom done by choice. These leaders grow from the coping mechanisms used to deal with tragedy. As failure conditions are identified, the leader develops rules for avoidance that are taught to a team. If even a small amount of utility is derived from a rule, it becomes codified in the team's collective thinking and actions until tyranny exists in the thinking of each member of the team. After deposing a tyrant, a team member can easily step up as the "new" leader. Some rules change to match the new leader's failure avoidance tactics. Tyranny survives the destruction of the leader but accomplishes no cause. I would counsel against a loss-prevention strategy as a good method for short-circuiting pride.

Largesse

The most effective method for short-circuiting pride is to give someone else credit for the accomplishment. More to the point, give the whole team credit. No one person accomplishes a cause. Individuals on the team will contribute their efforts, but only as everyone participates will the vision be fulfilled, and the cause realized.

These contributions include the contributions of the leader, who is just another team member. The leader may have a uniquely important role in creating the ultimate victory, but their contribution is no more necessary than any other member of the team. During my time in the navy, I learned to never let people thank me for doing my job. Leaders are supposed to lead. Leading is not more praiseworthy and should therefore not be a source of excessive pride.

Taking on this attitude of individual contribution to the team effort is a powerful way to short-circuit pride. The leader's contribution gets the team organized and motivated. This coming together does not happen without the leader, but the accomplishment of the cause does not happen without the team. Leader and team are codependent if the world is to be changed. Why should the leader take pride in the vision's accomplishment more than the team? Unique as their contribution seems, the leader is only doing their job. Some pride in a job well done is healthy as a motivator. Giving the team the rest of the credit will prevent that pride from replacing purpose.

David takes giving credit to others to the next level. Because he has chosen a purpose that makes God the center of his actions, he rightly gives God all the credit for any success. David's vision announcement lists God as the reason for his actions and lists God as the bringer of success. I believe this is an example of the "clean living" that my grandfather mentioned often.

Giving credit to God has the added benefit of being able to explain the nature of tragedy without the need for a long list of failure conditions to avoid. David expected nothing but good outcomes if God was responsible for what happened. Later in his life, he would write about it:

Deliver me not over unto the will of mine enemies: for false witnesses are risen up against me, and such as breathe out cruelty. I had fainted, unless I had believed to see the goodness of the LORD in the land of the living. (Psalm 27:12, 13)

He learned to take even the tragedy of an enemy's successes against him as events ordained by God for the best possible outcome. As a result, he never wasted time making pointless rules.

A leader like David, who is dedicated to discovering and doing the right thing based on God's estimation of right, is not less likely to encounter tragedy. If God is the cause of all the events that befall a leader, then God is always responsible for the outcomes of those events. Leaders like David discover from careful study that God is working to bring about the best outcomes:

For I know the thoughts that I think toward you, saith the LORD, thoughts of peace, and not of evil, to give you an expected end. (Jeremiah 29:11)

Sometimes we may perceive outcomes as tragic, but if they resulted from the leader doing the right thing, then God is working on the "expected" end. This reliance on God's goodwill toward all, that can only be experienced by those who do the right thing, is a powerful tool for short-circuiting pride.

Promise

Your team is waiting to see if you will follow through on your promises. A reputation for accomplishing your promises queues up team members who are ready to act on the heels of accomplishment. Making appropriate promises helps ensure their participation. When making a promise, leaders should avoid claims of outcomes that will happen. Effective leaders promise actions that will be taken. Remember that predicting the future is not possible, so promised outcomes are not within a leader's control. Only your future actions are within your control, so limit your promises to those.

Though David asserted God as the cause for success, he declared actions that he promised to take to accomplish the cause of removing the reproach. David promised, "I will smite thee, and take thine head from thee" (1 Samuel 17:51). The Israeli army is now watching to see if he will follow through on those promises. "Therefore David ran, and stood upon the Philistine, and took his sword, and drew it out of the sheath thereof, and slew him, and cut off his head therewith. And when the Philistines saw their champion was dead, they fled" (1 Samuel 17:51). Only by completing the promised actions can David get the Israeli army to act.

Before engaging in the first action on the path to completing your cause, consider the next step. What action are you going to take next so that your team can see a pattern in you that convinces them that you will follow through on promises? Announcing that second action before attempting the first action is a great way to develop a sense of urgency in your team. They will act quickly if they see you live up to your reputation.

Gaining a good reputation is deliberate and one of the most valuable commodities a leader can possess. "A good name is rather to be chosen than great riches, and loving favour rather than silver and gold" (Proverbs

22:1). A disciplined approach to purposeful living is the only way I have discovered to build this quality reputation. Even when you encounter people who are willing to speak out against that reputation, you can silence those voices by living up to the reputation. Make a promise of future action that you plan to take, and when the time comes for that action, act.

Your team does not want to see that you are one of them. While one more person who believes and acts as they do would certainly grow the size of the team, they are not getting anywhere. Having a cause to fulfill grows from a unique perspective that seeks to change the world. They want to see that you live up to an ideal. If you act according to a good reputation and let nothing detour you from that pursuit, your idealistic actions become archetypal in the team's estimation. You can become the hero of your story.

Be careful that you do not set out to become a hero though. You want to live up to your reputation for taking the necessary actions. You do not need to promote, explain, qualify, or defend those actions. Declaring yourself to be the hero will not inspire a team to follow your lead. "Let another man praise thee, and not thine own mouth; a stranger, and not thine own lips" (Proverbs 27:2). Creating your own mythology is a surefire way to lose the support of your team.

Being a hero without becoming a myth is the tricky part. Even David would have his deeds mythologized by the nation of Israel. They wrote songs about him and even placed items of his in the sanctuary. "And the priest said, The sword of Goliath the Philistine, whom thou slewest in the valley of Elah, behold, it is here wrapped in a cloth behind the ephod: if thou wilt take that, take it: for there is no other save that here" (1 Samuel 21:9). David's battle with Goliath turned him into a mythological hero, but that began with a good reputation. Seek only to manage the reputation and avoid the myth wherever possible.

Make a promise. Do what you promised. Continue forward with confidence that you have finished the job and your team will now join you to complete the cause.

Panic

While preparing for success, take some extra time to figure out how to not panic. Panic is an overwhelming sense of fear and anxiety that leads to actions based on emotion instead of reason. A crisis emotional state replaces circumspection. This is an emotional state created by wrong thinking about unpredictable future events. Changing the emotion is as simple as changing the thinking, but some preparation can go a long way to short-circuiting the panic.

Panic arises easily in the aftermath of dramatic change. Change created by another leader may suddenly impact your cause, or the achievement of the first announced action may shift the risk profile significantly. These sudden changes open new possibilities for disaster that were not known before the change event. Because we tend to be so heavily tilted toward avoiding negative consequences, all new possibilities suddenly seem overwhelming. Any effort made to reevaluate the situation expands the potential for negative results and deepens the fear. Panic becomes cyclical, and soon all actions are reactions to forestall potential negative consequences, rather than all actions being focused on a cause.

Knowing that panic is a relevant possible result of success may not be enough to prevent panic. When the first successful action is completed and the risk evaluation changes, panic becomes a possible response. Instead of carefully executing a preset plan, the leader begins acting erratically to avoid damage from the new risks. Panic causes the leader to set aside circumspection for immediate action, and those actions are not likely to align with the leader's purpose.

Because OODA is primarily utilized when unexpected events happen, it can be used in these moments of risk revaluation as well. In fact, any pre planned patterns of analysis can be more useful in these moments than the leader's original plans. The leader's actions have changed the risk profile that informed the original plan, changing the plan's relevance. Any pattern of analysis that circumspectly assesses the new risk profile can help align an immediately necessary action with the leader's purpose. Leaders who are prepared with a patterned response do not need complete plans. Like David, who ran to take Goliath's head without taking a sword, these leaders can quickly evaluate the situation and make an appropriate second, third, and fourth action that were not a part of the original plan.

The problem with panic is the "unthinking behavior." Leaders who allow emotion or instinct to determine their next action are no longer keeping their purpose at the forefront. This would be equivalent to David running back to the Israeli army for support or charging the Philistine front line before finishing the job. In the moments between the first success and finishing the job, successful leaders think. Quick thoughts perhaps, but at the very least recommitting a purpose that led to success. Next actions are aligned with that purpose, and no room is made for panic.

Because of the tragic nature of life, many people have developed panic into a refined response choice. These people typically fit into the simpleton or fool category that requires special handling from the leader. They have developed panic to a pathological degree and are completely dependent on it for all of their actions. Purpose has been replaced in them with a keen sense of the possible tragedies that might happen next, and all actions are immediately driven by this anticipation. While tragedy is not prevented, these reactionaries will have a long list of tragedies that they claim were prevented by their actions. If potential team members are impressed with those supposed successes, they may decide to follow this person. Tyrants are easily created this way.

Panic-driven people are very active, though their actions do not conform to any attempt to create a cause or live a purpose. Each completed action creates an emergency situation where tragedy permeates their thinking and immediate action to forestall tragedy drives the next action. Each newly expected tragedy is assumed to be real and highly likely. Most of these imagined tragedies will never mature, regardless of the leader's actions. Nevertheless, actions become proof that the tragedy was imminent, and their lack becomes proof that the actions were relevant. This circular reasoning creates what appears to be an individual that the world would label as "type A," but they are just busy, not productive.

Safety becomes the objective and purpose for any leader acting in panic. These leaders assume that safety is the absence of tragedies, especially those avoided by the leader's actions. Tragedies still happen to these leaders and, unfortunately for the followers, are often attributed to someone not following the rules. Previous safety is proof of future safety if the team follows the leader's rules. Since panic is what drives the actions, it replaces reason and becomes purpose.

Avoiding the panic pitfall requires deliberate attempts to restore reason. This process starts simply. Don't panic! Refusing to have any emotional response to immediate events leaves the leader free to orient fully. Ask a binary question, "Is the cause completed?" Orient on the obstacles that remain to be overcome. Pull out a checklist of promises made in the vision statement and see what remains to be done. Decide on an action that will remove one or more of the obstacles or complete a promise. Act. Purpose and cause remain the driving forces.

Being ready to short-circuit pride, fulfil every promise, and do it without panic represents the ultimate success as a leader. David's thinking remains a mystery, but his actions are clear and simple. Samuel does not mention a fist pump, hoot, or end zone dance. David is in his place, doing the work, and using what he knows to complete a cause. Goliath's head must be taken to fulfill the promises made, so he gets busy doing that. He finishes the job because he was prepared for success.

PRECEPTS

- Prepare for success.
- Finish the job.

9

---◆---

MOVE OUT OF THE WAY

I got the call about one o'clock that a backhoe operator had ignored the markings on the street and dug up our service lines. This was a larger than normal tragedy. My team was spread across five hundred miles of desert, and the broken service was two hours from me. I contacted Ron, my second in command, and he headed back to the office to grab materials and tools for a repair, while I redirected the other four members of my service team and recruited expert assistants from a neighboring district. By the time I arrived on the scene, Ron had locked off the service to 120 customers, notified local authorities of the repair timeline, and was in the hole expanding the area we had to work in. I grabbed a shovel and jumped in.

I finally nudged Ron out of my way so that I could get a closer look at the damage and work on making the hole larger. Other team members arrived and watched me dig since there was no room in the hole for more workers. After about five minutes, Ron suggested that I needed to source a compressor to assist with completing the repairs, and he took my shovel from my hands while I used my cell phone.

When I set my phone down after finding a compressor, I discovered that the hole was full of my team. There were no tools for me and no room to use them if I could find one. They ignored me and continued working on solving the problem. I went to get the compressor. When I returned, I watched them work for a while, then ran a conference call with regional management and safety about our response to this little tragedy. I spent some time answering emails and watching the dirt fly.

As the sun set, I went to get dinner for the team. By the time I got a good, clear look at the damage, my team was eating dinner, and the expert was in the hole using tools that I was not familiar with. I watched, asked questions, and retrieved supplies but was concerned that I was not leading the team. They returned from eating, filled the hole with their presence, and sent me to make some more phone calls.

I had work to do for the day like any other workday in the office. I spent some time answering more emails. Then I worked on adjusting schedules for the next day to accommodate this emergency repair. By the time I returned to the hole, the repairs were complete. The team had paired up and taken on the tasks of testing and service restoration. I was not given a partner to work with, so I waited for them to finish.

I thought, *What a fine example of leadership you are, standing around watching while your team does all the work*. Of course! That is what should happen. They only needed me to set the vision and lead the way by heading to the emergency. If I was willing to go on-site, then they were too. My role as the leader was completed when I arrived on-site. After that, I just needed to get out of the way.

For more than a year, my team had been working together each morning on our conference calls to consider and discuss safety, logistics, and emergency responses. By the time the call came from the backhoe operator that afternoon, the team was prepared to do the work. I had done my job by reviewing the procedures, iterating the policies, and keeping everyone focused on doing the work safely. Getting the best result required me to point to the problem and then get out of the way. This can be a hard thing to do for a guy with dirt under his fingernails and calluses on his hands. As the leader, my job was to lead. Their jobs were to work in unison to build the solution, and though I knew the work, had done the work, and could do the work, it was not mine to do.

Realizing for the first time that my most important contribution was to get out of the way was unsettling in many ways. My first reaction was to return to familiar work and put my hands on a shovel. Next, I simply watched, which may seem like the wrong action, but it allowed my team to sort out the work that was required without feeling like they needed my approval for each decision. Finally, I began looking for ways to facilitate their work. The pattern was clear after the fact, but at that moment, I struggled with my role as the leader and felt like I no longer had one. Now, I expect to work through this simple pattern of behavior once my team gets involved: work, watch, wait.

WORK

My team did not need me to tell them what to do. This is often one of the hardest parts of filling the role of leader on the team. My assessment of the work is not necessarily better than my least experienced team member's assessment. That team member works with this unique problem every day and is much better qualified to make a decision. Giving instructions to a widget operator when I have never operated a widget is unwise. I had to let my team do what they knew to do.

That does not mean I did not have a role to play in leadership. My initial efforts got the team on-site, and they needed only to know what part of the situation needed attention. When I arrived, the hole was not big enough to work in. I decided to fix that before working on anything else, so I grabbed a shovel. My moving dirt with a shovel only showed my team where to find the immediate need for action. When they arrived, they saw where I was standing and what I was doing and got busy doing likewise. I did not tell anyone to get into the hole and dig.

The other interesting thing that happened is that Ron received time to think and develop a plan of action. Because I was acting as an example to get people busy, he was able to sequence the job and discover what resources might still be needed. Ron was quite capable of doing this job without me. So, I gave him the time to think by doing the work that was the least complicated and initially most critical. The team completed the service restoration by following his plan, not mine.

This was confusing at first, since I thought I was supposed to be the leader. Understanding this took most of the two-hour drive back home (and more than a year of reflection) to sort out. My team needed a plan to execute, and Ron was the best qualified to build that plan. Members of the team had warned me over the last year that if I was not careful, Ron would take my job. That night, I discovered that this was exactly what I wanted. My focus needed to remain on my purpose and promoting the causes that had nothing to do with this emergency.

Restoring the service for our customers was a needful event, but it was not a world-changing moment. Most of the work I do as a leader is related to keeping a team solving the emergencies of the moment. These are the little tragedies that pop up throughout the day and threaten to disrupt the cause by changing the world in a different direction. In the past, I have arrived at the decision point where eliminating the tragedies seems the only way to free up the time needed to work on a cause. Following that course eventually leads to a list of rules designed to prevent the conditions that lead to tragedy but leaving no room for a cause.

I believe this is the one aspect of leadership that confounds most efforts to see a cause realized. A leader steps out front with a cause to pursue and becomes enamored with the team members who sign up without hesitation. Team members stand around needing something to do. To get the ball rolling, the leader gives some instructions and is pleased when they are carried out. This leads to more instructions and eventually orders, until the leader spends their entire day giving orders instead of leading. Eventually, leaders replace purpose with the need to tell people what to do and have them do it. Power becomes the focus instead of purpose.

The biggest danger of pursuing the path of order giving is the need for discipline when orders are not carried out. This discipline typically deteriorates from a productive reorganizing of a team member's orientation to the cause into a more fruitless punishment for breaking a rule. The punishment is not designed to move the cause forward but to discourage the team member, or anyone else, from engaging in that activity again. If the behavior in question is an independent decision that the team member made, then the change will be that they quit making decisions. When they stop making decisions, they can now only receive and respond to orders, which the leader now must continually provide.

In the next chapter, we will see what that power-driven leadership scenario looks like, but for now, we can examine one way that a leader prevents this slow descent. First, do the simplest work only. When responding to a tragedy, find some simple and immediately necessary work to do. Your team needs an idea of where to find the problem, not to be told what to do to solve it. Second, the leader should allow another team member to be responsible for the plan. I would recommend not even indicating to the team who the plan maker should be; they can figure it out (in a true emergency where lives and property are at stake, do not leave this to chance but quickly identify who is responsible for the plan). Third, the leader has work that is necessary outside of the response to the tragedy, and that is the work that the leader should do. This frees up a team to make decisions about dealing with the tragedy and frees the leader to focus on the cause according to a purpose.

WATCH

People are strange in that we always perform better when someone is watching. This aspect of pride is one of the simplest motivators available to a leader. Team members will do their work faster, with higher quality, and with a greater sense of accomplishment if the leader is watching. This will not be a true statement if the leader comments critically on how the work is proceeding.

Watching is a passive activity that requires no comment while the work is going on. Standing around a large hole while my team worked to make it bigger felt awkward. As a member of the team, I could offer suggestions like, "Would a digging bar help break up that clay?" Every team member was expected to provide that sort of insight. What my team did not need was me giving a lesson on the ideal way to hold a shovel; this was not the time. All I could do was watch.

Learn instead of attempting to teach in these moments. As in this emergency response, my typical role as the team leader requires teaching how to respond to tragedy. Once the tragedy happens, my role changes to that of the learner. Was all of that instruction time productive? Is the team ready to deal with the tragedy because of that instruction? Insinuating myself into the work or the plan by giving instructions would not allow me to discover my team's level of preparedness. More importantly, I would have missed seeing all of the unique techniques that each member of the team employed. Yes, it is possible to learn more about how to dig a hole.

While I watched, my team worked, and I thanked them. Not profusely, but I made the rounds and personally thanked each team member for their quick response to this tragedy. I asked about their plans that needed to change to allow them to be there and apologized for the necessity. After the job was done, I commended each person both privately and publicly for their reliable response. What I did not communicate were any instructions or orders about how to do the work. I watched.

I avoided hovering though. Standing in one spot out of earshot and watching while talking on the phone has a tendency to inspire uneasy speculation in the team. When I took a call, I either did so from the side of our growing hole, or I left the site. While I knew I would be waiting for many hours, I made sure to stay in motion when in the presence of my team and to work quickly when I was not so that I could return. All these choices were circumspectly executed because I wanted each member of the team to see this as a success to be remembered for the rest of their lives. My plan did not set this moment aside as world-changing, but it could be an opportunity to unite, build, and improve the team to be ready for that plan.

WAIT

The work will take as long as it takes. Getting irritated about the late hour or the need for many more days of effort will not resolve the tragedy sooner. My team would be fighting through that desire to be irritated at eating a cold sandwich for dinner when a hot fried chicken dinner was on the table at home. They needed an example of a leader who never once mentioned a missed dinner, complained about the coming lack of sleep, or lamented over the long ride home. All I could do was wait.

Many times, in life, I arrived on the scene to find the work going slower than I expected. Instead of waiting, I jumped in to stop work for a lecture. I delivered my inspirational speech with confidence my team would shift into overdrive to get the work done faster. They returned to work confused about why I stopped them in the first place and wasted time talking. After the less-than-inspiring rhetoric, I would give new instructions that reorganized the effort.

In my opinion-of-the-moment, the newly organized work would reduce the workload, increase synergies, and get the job done quicker than anyone could imagine. Another half hour would expire while the team moved around, discussed the legitimacy of the new plan, and slowly started back to work. Work would proceed awkwardly while the newly paired team members adjusted to the rhythm of their partner. While work would continue, the team would shift to a more low-geared effort punctuated by frequent jokes, stories of recent fishing trips, and discussions of last night's football game. The team worked but not at their best. I continued giving orders, which my team tried hard to ignore until I was reduced to offering the occasional ignored suggestion.

Back then, I misunderstood the power of a proper delegation. A proper delegation gives authority and responsibility to team members in advance of the tragedy. Stopping the work for my speech established me as the party responsible. Giving orders demonstrated that I had the authority. I relieved my team of the need to make decisions. While these tragedies did get corrected, the work took longer than anticipated, and I could not get any of my work done because I was busy giving orders. I learned the hard way to wait while my team fixes the tragedy.

Leaders need to expect their team to make workable decisions, and causes fail when leaders are not willing to let them do so. In these moments of response to a tragedy, everyone looks to the leader, expecting orders. When they receive none, they should simply get busy doing what the leader has prepared them to do. At that moment, they look at each other and begin developing decision-making mechanisms to move the job forward faster and more efficiently. The team's decisions build a successful tragedy response or cause, not the leader's orders.

My patience paid off that night to get the service restored two hours ahead of my expectations. At the end of the job, we gathered to review any safety questions and share observations about how the job went. Everyone was tired, and no one complained about the long drive ahead of them across the empty, dark desert. Each member contributed key insights, and we all learned something new about emergency response, team dynamics, and the art of digging a hole. I thanked each team member for something specific that I had seen them contribute during our work, and I let everyone know where to find their revised schedules for tomorrow. I rescheduled the morning conference call for eight o'clock so everyone could sleep in. We left the job site with a sense of a completed task well done.

MOVE

David worked to promote the cause and completed the initial response by killing Goliath. His announced vision included the total destruction of the Philistine army though, and he was one man. Getting the Israeli army moving did not require any instructions from David. He gave no more speeches, issued no orders, and Samuel mentions no battle cries. Samuel tells us only that the army got busy after seeing David finish his work.

And the men of Israel and of Judah arose, and shouted, and pursued the Philistines, until thou come to the valley, and to the gates of Ekron. And the wounded of the Philistines fell down by the way to Shaaraim, even unto Gath, and unto Ekron. (1 Samuel 17:52)

Responses to a tragedy like the broken service line resemble causes in the manner that a team unites and responds together. An observer would see what looks like a carefully choreographed action that gives the impression of a team following orders. But a team following orders is limited by the number of unilateral decisions the leader makes. Technically speaking, the team should not be under the leader's control. The team should be empowered by clear delegation, allowing each autonomous team member to make decisions and take actions independent of unique leadership control. Properly trained and led team members make decisions and act according to their estimation of what it means to do the right thing.

Tragedy responses and causes reach tipping points that ensure that the events that follow are not under the direct control of the leader anyway. The team is the mechanism needed to finish a cause that changes the world. If everyone knows their place, their people, and their purpose (in this case the vision), then they will act without any more input from the leader when the time arrives for action. If the leader is successful in completing the initial steps announced for the cause, then the team will take over if the leader moves out of the way.

The movement does not need to be announced. When my team was busy digging, they really did not care where I was or what I was doing. They saw me on-site when they arrived, and I was busy working. Letting them know that I would be on a call with regional management about their work would not have added anything to the effort of digging. Declaring, "I am going to get out of the way now and stand over there," would have set me up to receive constant interruptions as team members stopped work to see if I approved of the latest decision. Instead, I quietly stepped back and moved away.

Often in the past, I would step in to utilize every motivational and instructional moment that I could create. Lecturing a digging team member on the relative differences between digging in sand or clay adds only comic relief. Pulling a team member aside for a serious conversation about his possession motivator only slows the work. Any adjustments that need to be made to someone's motivational mix can wait till the emergency or world-changing cause is complete. Professional athletes do not stop in the middle of a championship game to spend a few minutes reviewing and practicing the basics.

Samuel had nothing more to say about how David performed through the ensuing battle. The battle takes two sentences, and David is not mentioned at all. Most noteworthy though, he now carries a head that could weigh as much as thirty pounds, if he removed the brass helmet. Samuel pushes past the battle to find David being ushered into Saul's presence with Goliath's head in hand. Running at the enemy lines with their champion's head in his hand would have been terrifying but not wise since the sword in his other hand was made for a giant to carry. David's actions during the battle are not mentioned because the leader is only part of the team whose actions get the battle started. The team, not the leader, finishes the fight.

World-changing causes begin with a leader and end with the team's actions. David's purpose revealed a cause. He chose to lead, acquired a delegation, and announced the vision. Hitting Goliath with the stone disrupted the patterns that the world had become accustomed to. Removing Goliath's head was the tipping point that activated the team to action. When that moment arrived, David needed only to move out of the way.

Completing a cause or responding to tragic events requires the same approach to work. The leader's efforts build the cause and recruit the team. After reaching the tipping point, the leader moves out of the way, and the team does the work. David's team changed the balance of power in the Middle East that day and every day since. The Philistines did not go away, but Israel now had a leader who could make up for their ineffective king. All David did was move out of the way.

PRECEPTS

- Move out of the way.

10

———◦———

POWER

Effective leaders are driven by purpose or power. My original intent was to discuss only the purpose-driven model of leadership and not discuss the power-driven model. However, the story of David and Goliath ends with an example of what will happen to a purpose-driven leader in a power-driven hierarchy. Understanding how to navigate within that power hierarchy to acquire authority, accomplish your cause, and do so without being consumed in someone's agenda would be a useful skill set. Please do not read into this that I approve of or recommend the power-driven model. I advise against even beginning to build a power base.

The power-driven model can be effective from the perspective of growing a team. Even a significantly delusional tyrant can hold a team together for a lifetime by delivering team members' motivational ideas. The seduction for the follower is that the powerful leader seems to protect the interests of their followers and advance their follower's agendas. Growing a power base requires fulfilling some of the motivational ideas of followers to inspire reciprocity. The expectation is that the team member whose motivational idea has been realized by the leader's intervention will submit unwavering loyalty to follow orders without question. This arrangement of special privilege in exchange for complete loyalty is the archetypal "making a deal with the devil."

Power-driven leaders gather a small team around them, pull them in tight by promising to protect their interest, and then avoid conflict. They withhold all authority, responsibility, and accountability. While few decisions will or can be made, these leaders are not interested in seeing effective decisions made to create change. They want crafty decisions that avoid conflict and grow their power base. They do not drive their teams into conflict unless they encounter an opportunity to grow their power base and the increase in power is sufficient to offset the risks. They comfort themselves with the idea that if something goes wrong, they can leverage their power to correct it while sacrificing only a few team members. Ultimately, all followers are disposable and can be offered up as sacrifice if such sacrifice protects or increases the power base.

Gathering and keeping team members requires a delicate balance of bribery and threats of violence. Team members typically join because the leader is able to help them realize a motivational idea. For their effort, the leader expects reciprocity in the form of loyalty.

LOYALTY

Loyalty is the hallmark of these bottom-up organizations, and betrayal is met with the most severe violence. While the internal language of loyalty will imply loyalty to the team, in truth, loyalty attaches to the leader and is not reciprocal. After satisfying that first motivational idea, the leader is not likely to waste power on additional motivational ideas and will resort to threats of violence to provide the leverage that may be needed to move team members to act. Team members who want to stay in the leader's good graces perform their assigned tasks but never seek to make decisions. Even if a threat to their personal safety requires immediate action, team members seek permission from the leader before acting.

PERMISSION

Permission replaces delegation as the empowering characteristic of a power-driven leader. In a delegation, the leader gives authority and responsibility to allow the delegate to make decisions, while the leader retains accountability. In a power-driven team, the delegate becomes a supplicant who brings a decision to the king and asks for permission to take action. If the king agrees, he gives permission, which is the authority, responsibility, and *accountability* to act in this one narrow decision.

BRIBE

These leaders value success in accomplishing the defined result only if the success also grows the power base. Good success in growing the power base can be rewarded with the realization of additional motivational ideas. Often the rewards are well in excess of what would be expected as reciprocal for success in the endeavor, because it is based on the side effect of increasing the leader's power base. For the leader, success is always defined as a growth in power, with no concern for the success of any cause. In fact, failure in a cause that leads to an increase in the leader's power would still be seen as a success. Success in a cause that negatively impacts the power base brings punishment.

PUNISHMENT

Power-driven leaders reward success (increased power) mightily, but there are always strings attached that leave the reward under the leader's control so that they can remove it as a form of punishment. Team members who regularly increase the power base will thrive well beyond their more average teammates, but they could also be the next sacrifice. Trappings of success—car, nice office, upscale memberships, access to corporate retreats—may seem like rewards, but supplicants who waver at doing what they are told will see these benefits removed to force compliance.

MORE POWER

Power-driven teams tend to continue growing if the leader maintains the balance of bribes and punishment. The leader must continually pursue power secretly as an agenda. The leader does not tie the team down with a clear vision because they want the team nimble enough to shoot for the short-term goals that increase the leader's power base. Increases in power can come from above, through delegations or permissions, but most often come from below as additional team members are added.

While everyone on the team will be busy, they will not be clear about a unified objective. In modern business, these leaders often purchase posters with dramatic pictures with a single word that are reported to encapsulate the vision. I have been in organizations where this one-word wish fulfillment is taken up a notch with three to five words that are referred to as the company's core values. The company's core values are typically codified over a multiyear plan to have management redefine what it means to be *one of us*. These words are always aspirational but not well defined. Even for those members of the team who understand and attempt to apply these core values, their application by management will be inconsistent because they are not backed by a leader's purpose. These core value statements keep management busy trying to force compliance, leaving the leader to pursue their agendas. The leader's core values never reflect those announced for the team.

DANGER

Supplicants who bring innovative ideas to the leader may obtain permission. Even a purpose-driven leader can gain authority this way and may create real change as a result, but the power-driven king gave permission because he saw an opportunity to strengthen his power base. If you are that purpose-driven supplicant, be ready for the possible negative consequences of your success.

Remember, when you go to the king, you want his authority to act. Effective leaders assume responsibility and accountability, but these are made explicit with permission. Power-driven followers seldom approach the king for permission because they have already surrendered responsibility and authority to the king and are now waiting to be told what to do. So, the very act of asking the king for his permission draws the king's full attention to that leader.

A leader's willingness to step forward to create change could be a threat to the king's power base. While permission comes with the needed authority, it will also contain an element of risk that the king will begin an investigation into what he perceives as the leader's power base—an action that is typically only taken when someone of equal power is encountered. Unfortunately, the result of the investigation will be disastrous for the purpose-driven leader because the best possible outcome is a cautious paranoia from the king, and the worst is immediate violence.

Pursuing power as a purpose is a zero-sum game where the submitted followers lose as they surrender power to the leader they are following. Followers in these teams can regain power under their leader by finding their own followers who will surrender their power, giving rise to the typical power hierarchy that is predominant in the world. The harder a leader works at building power, the more power they take from others. The strong (or lucky) survive, the weak cower, and the tyrants attempt to take over the world.

Rarely will you encounter a king who is not entangled in a power hierarchy. In chapter 15 of 1 Samuel, we find the account of Saul being given instructions from God to destroy the Amalekites. Saul used this war as an opportunity to build a power base with the people by allowing them to profit from the spoils, which was expressly forbidden by God. Saul abandoned his purpose of following God's instructions and began building a power hierarchy with himself at the top. At the end of the chapter, after Samuel has told Saul that he no longer has God's favor, all Saul cares about is Samuel coming with him to worship God before the people. In so doing, Samuel is validating Saul before the people and solidifying Saul's power base. Loss of his purpose was unimportant to Saul if he could maintain and grow his power.

David took appropriate action within that power hierarchy to gain permission (authority) to act against Goliath. Though he acts on Saul's behalf and with Saul's permission, he becomes a target. If David had died in his efforts, then Saul could easily have held the dead man accountable, but his victory allowed David to rally Saul's army to act. Saul's power base did not abandon him, since it was his permission that allowed David to act, but if David, who already assumed responsibility, attempted to lead the army without permission, they were likely to follow. Since most of Saul's power base was in that army, David was now a threat.

David already had the authority from God's anointing through Samuel. I mention this because while you may not need to approach a power-driven king for permission, they may come to you offering their assistance. This happened to Nehemiah when he was rebuilding the walls of Jerusalem. As the power-driven kings in the local area saw Nehemiah's success in rebuilding the city walls, they sought to create a time of peace during which they could negotiate and decide how best to share power. Nehemiah refused to engage in this discussion, recognizing that his authority came from God. His purpose-backed cause received his attention instead of the power hierarchy that meant to destroy him.

POWER CONFLICTS

Power as a purpose has a massive downside. All power-driven leaders eventually encounter another leader who is more powerful. These are highly charged encounters with some predictable outcomes. During the first meeting, each will recognize the power ambitions of the other. Recognition will inspire immediate investigations to identify the stronger. These investigations conclude with one of the leaders deciding they are the more powerful, which creates the inevitable conflict.

There may be instances where the leaders you are forced to follow are engaged in power building, and you may need to protect your team from the fallout of these conflicts, so we should look at some possible outcomes. Unfortunately for David, Saul was committed to building his power base. Conflict with David's purpose-driven leadership was inevitable.

Saul already has decided to begin an investigation to discover what David's power base looks like. Concluding that he is the more powerful, Saul will act to remove the threat that David represents and, if possible, collect his followers and the power they represent. Saul fears that David might have enough power to overthrow him, which is a real and present threat in any power hierarchy.

Saul's investigation begins with an unassuming enough question, "And when Saul saw David go forth against the Philistine, he said unto Abner, the captain of the host, Abner, whose son is this youth? And Abner said, As thy soul liveth, O king, I cannot tell" (1 Samuel 17:55). As I read this verse in sequence with the previous chapters, my suspicion was that Samuel's visit to Jesse's house was not a secret. Samuel was God's prophet and Saul's mentor, so the king would be obsessively interested in what the prophet was doing. The prophet represented a threat since he was not a submitted part of Saul's power base. While Saul may have known where Samuel was and what he did while there, some of the details are not present, like the name of the newly anointed king. All Saul might have known about Samuel's activities was that one of Jesse's sons had been anointed, but Saul would not necessarily know who Jesse was since he was too old to be a part of the army.

Detente

Having a power-driven leader investigate your power base is a dangerous moment for any leader. Most often, this is accomplished through an arranged period of detente to allow for "open" discussions for "mutual" benefit. Rational discourse identifies areas of mutual benefit for collaboration that loosely joins the two organizations. The two power hierarchies are merged, and a short battle is fought for control of the new power structure.

Saul has the best chance of winning the battle for control of the conjoined hierarchy because he started from a more powerful position. David has only two options, submitting his power to Saul or fighting for control. But because Saul is the more powerful, he gets to choose which of those choices David can make, and noncompliance would be grounds for immediate hostile action. In situations where one of the leaders is more powerful and can demonstrate an ability to protect the less powerful leader, then submission is a likely outcome. If the leaders possess equivalent power, they will fight until one of the two leaders is destroyed.

Battle

Any detente discussions will produce a battle opportunity that is heavily weighted in favor of one of the leaders. This tactic is evidenced in the valley of Elah with the Israeli and Philistine armies. For forty days, the armies have been experiencing a strange time of detente as Goliath lays out a battle plan that should have an obvious conclusion. Since the Philistines have Goliath, they have the most certain power position. The best positioned leader is the most likely winner in these encounters but not always.

The plan backfires if the best positioned leader's investigators incorrectly evaluate the power base of the other. Most often, an investigator incorrectly evaluates the level of power inherent in what they determine to be an inconsequential part of the other leader's hierarchy. In the case of David and Goliath, the Philistines have determined that the God of Israel is irrelevant in the battle. David's devotion to God produced in him a willingness to confront blasphemy that far exceeded the estimation of the investigators. Arguably, David's God, or at least the cause promoted by David's purpose to please his God, changed the power balance, giving David the advantage in this battle.

Secret Weapon

Often the incorrect valuation of strength happens if a power-driven leader attempts to take over a cause-motivated team. Power-driven leaders are focused only on building more power and typically assume that all leaders do the same. Since the cause is not considered in the investigation, a circumspect purpose-driven leader who is focused on a cause can often prevail.

Purpose-driven leaders gain advantage by simply not playing the power acquisition game and focusing on doing the right thing according to their purpose. Power-driven leaders always underestimate the strengths that are created by this defined focus and overestimate their chances of prevailing. Purpose-driven leaders can blast through the power-driven structures building a team of converts. On rare occasions, the entire power structure is sucked up into the cause as the power-driven king is recruited as a team member.

A purpose-driven leader is less likely to accept the detente and much less likely to allow their team to be merged into another leader's power hierarchy. Only in cases where the cause requires the authority held by a power-driven leader will there be any common ground. Circumspect purpose-driven leaders may even choose a new cause rather than place their team under the tyranny of the power-driven king. To gain the king's authority requires submission. After submission, separating the team from the king's power base will require an act of insurrection.

Eventually, power-driven leaders force the issue, bringing conflict. Saul has little choice but to join David's team today because the Israeli army joined. Saul needs the army to solidify and maintain his power. Though Saul should be pleased with the outcome of David's battle, Samuel does not mention any words of praise. Instead, Saul wants an answer to the only question that remains for him, "Is David God's anointed?" Discovering the truth of this, Saul recognizes that David received from God the more powerful position in the hierarchy.

And when Saul saw David go forth against the Philistine, he said unto Abner, the captain of the host, Abner, whose son is this youth? And Abner said, As thy soul liveth, O king, I cannot tell. And the king said, Enquire thou whose son the stripling is. And as David returned from the slaughter of the Philistine, Abner took him, and brought him before Saul with the head of the Philistine in his hand. And Saul said to him, Whose son art thou, thou young man? And David answered, I am the son of thy servant Jesse the Bethlehemite. (1 Samuel 17:55–58)

THREATS

Saul now knows for certain that the new champion of Israel is also God's anointed king. Saul occupies the remainder of his life trying to have David killed. David submitted himself under Saul's leadership and would remain committed until Saul's death. Saul eventually makes David the leader of his army, but all his assignments are designed to be death traps. The power-driven king will never stop attempting to destroy the purpose-driven leader. Saul's irrational behavior eventually leads him to fall on his own sword in a moment of despair.

Rarely does a power-driven leader end otherwise. The larger their organizations grow, the more likely they are to be facing challenges to their authority from within. Growth of the power base leads to the destruction of the leader. Strangely enough, these destructive events happen frequently to the power-driven crowd, but we seldom hear about it since these leaders are not pursuing a cause that would change the world. The victorious leader steals the power base only to inevitably encounter a more powerful leader.

DEAD END

Pursuing power is a dead end. The world's current population of more than 8.5 billion climbs incessantly up these ever-shifting power hierarchies. Most people play the power game but never achieve the authority necessary to fulfill even one team member's motivational ideas. Survival as a power-driven leader means making it to the top of the heap and having everyone subject to destruction in your hands. Recruiting team members from lower on the hierarchy is simple enough, but to reach the top means toppling more powerful leaders—and not just one but a succession of more powerful leaders. Even if luck gets you halfway, there are still 4.25 billion opportunities for you to be crushed.

David demonstrates the only proper approach for the purpose-driven leader by staying committed to their purpose during the power conflict rather than attempting to destroy the king. Throughout his life, David had many occasions where hubris led to actions that were inconsistent with his purpose. His team, the nation of Israel, always suffered when he did. To his credit, David always repented when confronted with his sins. After public confessions, he would return to his purpose and continue his efforts to be a man after God's own heart.

Your purpose will be no different. At times, your dedication to it will lead to causes that change the world. When you encounter power-driven leaders and you remain true to your purpose in pursuit of a cause, the world will change. If your authority came from a power-driven leader, winning the cause necessitates an investigation into your power. Regardless of the outcome of that investigation, the power-driven leader will seek your destruction in a conflict that you cannot avoid. Destroy that leader to take their power, and eventually you will be that power-driven leader bent on your own destruction.

The decision math for the coming conflict is simple. Pursue power, and eventually, you lose it all. Pursue a purpose, and you can start the day with no power and no team, select a cause, consult a king, kill a giant, and change the world before the sun sets. Even if you lose your team in a power conflict, your purpose will remain intact. If you refuse power and simply return to your place and continue your work, another cause will surface. Stay true to your purpose.

PRECEPTS

- Stay true to your purpose.

www.ingramcontent.com/pod-product-compliance
Lightning Source LLC
Chambersburg PA
CBHW021412210526
45463CB00001B/340